Making Progress

to First Certificate

Teacher's Book

Leo Jones

CAMBRIDGE
UNIVERSITY PRESS

PUBLISHED BY THE PRESS SYNDICATE OF THE UNIVERSITY OF CAMBRIDGE
The Pitt Building, Trumpington Street, Cambridge, United Kingdom

CAMBRIDGE UNIVERSITY PRESS
The Edinburgh Building, Cambridge CB2 2RU, UK
40 West 20th Street, New York, NY 10011–4211, USA
477 Williamstown Road, Port Melbourne, VIC 3207, Australia
Ruiz de Alarcón 13, 28014 Madrid, Spain
Dock House, The Waterfront, Cape Town 8001, South Africa

http://www.cambridge.org

First published 2005
Printed in the United Kingdom at the University Press, Cambridge

Text typefaces Minion and Meta Plus Medium, System QuarkXpress® [HAR]

A catalogue record for this book is available from The British Library

ISBN 0 521 53702 9 Student's Book
ISBN 0 521 53703 7 Self-Study Student's Book
ISBN 0 521 53704 5 Teacher's Book
ISBN 0 521 53705 3 Workbook
ISBN 0 521 53706 1 Workbook with Answers
ISBN 0 521 53707 X Set of 2 audio cassettes
ISBN 0 521 53708 8 Set of 2 audio CDs

Cover design by Andrew Oliver
Produced by Hardlines Limited, Charlbury

Contents

Introduction

Making Progress is a course for students of all ages who aren't quite ready to begin a First Certificate preparation course using a course like *New Progress to First Certificate.* Students at this level need to consolidate their English language skills and become more confident in speaking ansd writing. *Making Progress* leads students up to the level required to begin an exam-directed course and covers the skills that they will need for the exam. There is no explicit FCE exam training in *Making Progress,* but all the needs of future exam candidates are dealt with.

Making Progress will help students to:

- become more fluent and confident in speaking
- develop their reading, writing and listening skills
- improve their grammar and vocabulary

Making Progress is also very suitable for students at mid-intermediate level who aren't going to take FCE. The activities and exercises provide an entertaining and worthwhile course for students who simply need to **make progress** at this level!

The **Student's Book** contains **24 units**, each in two parts: **A** and **B**. Each unit is based on a different topic, and each part covers a different aspect of the topic.

Part A contains three sections:

Speaking and vocabulary

Grammar practice

Vocabulary development or **Pronunciation**

Part B contains three sections:

Reading or **Listening**

Writing

Speaking

Each part contains enough material for one 60–90 minute lesson.

After every five units there is a **Revision** unit, which revises the vocabulary, grammar and pronunciation from the previous five units. There are puzzles and exercises to help students to remember what they learnt. These can all be done either as homework or in class – as you prefer.

How does each type of section work?

Part A
Speaking

Working in pairs or groups

The **Speaking** activities in *Making Progress* are most effective when learners work together in pairs or small groups of three to five students. The activities will help students to build up their confidence in speaking and continuing to speak in spite of their limited vocabulary and the grammatical mistakes they make.

The larger the class, the more these student-centred activities make sense because:

- they give everyone a chance to speak
- they allow meaningful conversations to develop, as opposed to isolated language practice
- they free learners from the fear of losing face in front of the whole class.

Discussions give students a chance to practise using English and help them to become more confident in speaking English. Remind students that it's important to use English all the time when they're working with partners – because the only way to improve their spoken English is by *speaking* it!

In some **Speaking** activities, called **Communication activities**, each person looks at different information. The **Communication activities** are printed on separate pages in the **Student's Book** (pages 131 to 143) so that students can't read each other's information and a natural conversation develops between them.

➡️ For more advice on working in pairs or groups, see the 'Extra teaching tips' section on page 9.

Challenging exercises

Some of the more open-ended activities in *Making Progress* are quite challenging. Students won't possess all the language they require to participate easily and fluently. There are several ways of getting around this problem, not all of which will be necessary at the same time:

- Quickly go through a few vocabulary items students can use in the activity
- Act out or demonstrate what has to be done
- Make sure students read through the role information carefully and ask questions before they begin (and as necessary during the activity)
- Remind students that in real life they won't have anyone to help them out and they'll have to cope by using their limited English resources in similar situations. The activities in this course will build their confidence in real-life situations.

Part A
Vocabulary

Your students are sure to want to find out more words to use in discussion about the topics that interest them most, so time must always be allowed for them to ask questions on vocabulary. Further vocabulary is introduced in the other sections in each unit and many of the words used in the **Vocabulary** exercise come up again.

As they work through *Making Progress*, students will be learning more and more vocabulary. Some items are presented in special **Vocabulary** exercises, while others occur in context in the recordings and the reading texts.

In the **Listening** exercises students may ask about other words that aren't printed in the **Student's Book**. For this reason, it's a good idea to preview the transcripts of the recorded material so as to be prepared to answer questions about any potentially difficult words. Highlight the words in the transcript in the **Teacher's Book** which you think your students need to know before they start listening.

You will discover that some of the vocabulary used in *Making Progress* is 'low-frequency', especially in the recordings. These may include words or expressions that are not often used in everyday conversation – but students should get used to encountering and coping with such low-frequency words. In many cases, they will be able to guess their meanings from the context.

In some exercises, students are expected to use dictionaries to look up the meanings of unfamiliar words. Any kind of dictionary is suitable for these exercises, even a small bilingual one, but I recommend that your students use an English-to-English dictionary. The best one for students at this level is the *Cambridge Learner's Dictionary*.

In *Making Progress* students are often asked to highlight words or phrases in their **Student's Book**. Highlighting vocabulary turns each person's book into an instant revision aid. Every time they look back at sections they have already done, the vocabulary they want to remember 'jumps out from the page', reminding them of the vocabulary items and showing the words in context. Just leafing back through previous units in a free moment (on the bus or standing in a queue, for example) will help them to revise vocabulary really easily.

What students should not do is highlight whole paragraphs of text (as if they were memorizing passages from a textbook for an exam). The selective approach of highlighting just a few chosen words on each page is much more effective.

➡ For more advice about helping students to learn vocabulary, see page 12.

In the **Workbook** there are more puzzles to help students to revise the topic vocabulary they've encountered in the **Student's Book**.

Part A
Grammar practice

The **Grammar practice** section in each unit is designed to revise the main problem areas of English grammar that students find tricky. Each set of exercises has an accompanying Grammar reference section at the back of the book (pages 118 to 130 of the **Student's Book**) with further examples and explanations of the basic rules. Students may refer to the Grammar reference sections before or after doing the exercises, or when revising on their own.

Students should realize that the **Grammar practice** sections provide revision of points that they have probably covered in previous courses. The summaries given in the Grammar reference pages are necessarily brief and simplified and do not cover elementary points or more advanced points. If students require more detailed rules or guidelines they should refer to a grammar reference book. Encourage your students to ask questions if they're unsure about any points in the Grammar reference section.

There are a variety of exercises to help students to become aware of grammatical rules and to become more accurate in their speech and writing. These include exercises where students are encouraged to discover different meanings, decide what is correct and incorrect, transform sentences, fill gaps with appropriate words and complete sentences.

In the **Workbook** there are more Grammar practice exercises.

Part A
Vocabulary development

These sections are designed to help students to consolidate what they already know about the important aspects of word-formation and vocabulary, enabling them to correct any errors they make and to widen their knowledge. The exercises in these sections can be done in pairs or by students working individually.

In the **Workbook** there are more exercises to help students with vocabulary development.

Part A
Pronunciation

These sections are designed to help students to improve their pronunciation of English sounds and use rhythm and intonation appropriately. The recordings provide some listening exercises and repetition exercises.

Part B
Listening

In **Part B** of each unit there is *either* a **Reading** section *or* a **Listening** section.

The purpose of the **Listening** exercises is to give students plenty of practice in listening to spoken English and to develop skills to make them better listeners. The tasks are designed to help them to understand the main points that are made – and discourage them from listening to every single word or worrying about the words they don't understand.

Some of the recordings are totally authentic and some are improvised so that they resemble English as it is actually spoken in a variety of realistic situations. The voices represent a variety of authentic accents, and the speech contains the normal hesitations, false starts, pauses and interruptions that occur in authentic spoken language. All these hesitations and false starts are reproduced in the transcripts.

➡ For more tips and advice on teaching listening skills, see page 13.

Part B
Reading

The **Reading** texts have questions to help students to understand them, learn more vocabulary and then discuss the topic.

Before the reading comprehension questions there are often preliminary discussion questions or some questions about the theme that students may be able to answer from their own previous knowledge. This task helps students to approach the text with more interest and curiosity than if they merely had to 'Read the text and answer the questions'.

In the **Workbook** there are lots more **Reading** texts. These are different in that they are longer and intended to be read for pleasure and interest. There is a glossary of difficult words. Recent research shows that reading purely for pleasure or information is one of the best ways of learning vocabulary. It's also a helpful way for students to improve their grammar and develop a good writing style.

➡ See page 14 for more tips and advice on dealing with **Reading** texts.

Part B
Writing

The **Writing** section in each unit covers a wide range of different aspects of writing compositions, letters and stories. Besides practice in the individual skills, students have longer composition tasks to encourage them to write in English and communicate their ideas to each other in writing.

Make sure you allow everyone time to read each other's written work. This is particularly important if composition writing is to be considered as more than 'just a routine exercise'. Any piece of writing should be an attempt to communicate ideas to a reader. If students know that their partners, as well as you, are going to read their work, they're more likely to try to make it interesting, informative and entertaining! If you, their teacher, are the only reader, the process of writing is much less motivating. Students can learn a lot from reading each other's ideas – and from each other's comments on their own work. What is most important is the success of a composition as a piece of communication, not simply its lack of grammatical errors.

➡ For a suggested marking scheme for written work, see page 15.

Part B
Speaking

At the end of each **Part B** there is a **Speaking** section. These activities cover different aspects of speaking in conversations and discussions, and expressing different functions. The speech balloons give students useful phrases to help them to speak in a clear, polite and friendly way, and many of these **Speaking** sections include pronunciation practice. The recording provides spoken models for the useful phrases in the speech balloons.

Repetition practice may at first seem a little childish to some students but it's an essential technique to help students to improve their pronunciation and build up their fluency and confidence. It's no good knowing useful phrases unless you can say them easily and confidently, and repeating in chorus is an enjoyable way of doing this.

Recordings

The recordings for *Making Progress* are available on CD or cassette.

Self-study Student's Book

Pages 144 to 187 in the Self-study edition contain answers to all the exercises and transcripts of the recordings.

Workbook

The *Making Progress* **Workbook** contains extra work on:

- Topic vocabulary
- Grammar
- Vocabulary development and pronunciation
- Reading passages for extensive reading, with a glossary explaining difficult words

There are two versions of the **Workbook**: one **With Answers** and one **Without Answers.**

I hope your students enjoy *Making Progress!*

Introduction

Extra teaching tips

A detailed description of the course is given in the Introduction. What follows here are general tips and advice for using *Making Progress*.

What's the teacher's role during pair or group work?

While students are working in pairs or groups, move around the class and listen to each pair or group for a few moments. If you think it would be helpful, join in occasionally and offer encouragement, advice, or suggestions. Make notes on any important mistakes you hear while you're walking around – but don't spend time actually correcting students' mistakes while they're trying to express themselves.

The teacher has three main responsibilities in getting students involved in pair or group work:

- getting things started (making sure everyone knows what to do and has the necessary vocabulary to do it – and telling them approximately HOW LONG the activity should take)
- monitoring the pairs or groups at work and deciding exactly when to stop the activity
- leading a short follow-up discussion after each activity (answering questions, pointing out significant mistakes and giving additional practice)

If your class doesn't have an even number of students, you may need to place some students in groups of three with two members of the group doing the same task. Rearrange pairs and groups frequently so that students are exposed to different speech styles and ideas. For some activities, you may want to place outgoing learners together so they don't intimidate others. In other situations, you may want the shy students paired with more outgoing partners so they can learn from them.

What if an activity doesn't seem to be working?

Don't worry if a **Speaking** activity fails to take off with a particular class. Open-ended exercises are inherently unpredictable. Bear in mind the attitudes and prejudices of your class when you are selecting activities and be prepared to 'sell' an activity to your students if you believe it to be a particularly worthwhile one. Some activities are easier than others. The ease with which students complete an activity may have more to do with the opinions, imagination, experience, versatility and knowledge they bring to class than with the level of English required for the activity. Above all, though, the activities are designed to be enjoyable so that students will be motivated to continue improving their English.

'Oh, no! Do we really have to work in pairs?'

👥 or 👥👥 Many of the exercises in *Making Progress* are designed to be done by students working together in pairs or in small groups of three or four. They're not designed to be quickly done 'round the class' with each student answering one question.

But some of your students may say to you:

'We don't like working in pairs or groups.'

'Pair work is fun, but what are we learning?'

'There are too many students in our class for group work.'

'We want you to listen to us and correct us whenever we make mistakes.'

Despite all the progress that has been made in language teaching in recent years, it still seems that some students prefer their teacher to lead them and guide them – or is it that they don't want to talk to each other? Anyhow, pair and group work doesn't seem to be popular with everyone.

Under such pressure from students, it may be tempting to reduce the emphasis on pair and group work. But, if anything, I believe there should be more emphasis. This is because pair and group work really is the most effective way (the only way?) to involve students in natural communication in English in the classroom – especially when the classroom is probably the *only* place they do speak English. In fact, the larger the class, the greater the need to work in pairs and groups – otherwise hardly anyone gets a chance to speak English in class.

For example, rather than have students working as individuals, it is preferable to do pair or group work in these situations:

- When students are doing a blank-filling exercise. Discussing the possible answers and trying to reach agreement is a really good way of using English to communicate ideas. The exchange of views between students, as they collaborate to get the answers right can easily lead to natural communication in English. In some ways, an exercise is quite similar to a problem-solving task: the students work together to 'solve' the exercise – possibly in competition with other pairs. This can be fun too! (This also works for reading comprehension exercises.)

- After doing a **Listening** exercise. Instead of simply going through the correct answers, allow time for the students to work in pairs to compare their answers. If there are any questions they couldn't answer, or any discrepancies between their answers, there's a strong motivation to want to listen to the recording again and find out who was right. This kind of discussion is an ideal opportunity for students to communicate with each other.

- After students have written a composition for homework, put them into small groups and ask them to read each other's work and comment on it.

- Discuss topics in small groups, not as a whole class. This gives more students a chance to give their opinions, rather than saying or thinking 'I agree with what she just said'. Many students feel shy about talking in front of the whole class and feel more relaxed and confident in a small group – and everyone can have their say without pressures of time or embarrassment.

Why is pair work and group work important?

Pair and group work is important because:

- Students get an opportunity to communicate their ideas to each other while they're discussing each exercise.

- Students are more likely to remember answers they have discovered or worked out by themselves than answers other students give – or answers the teacher announces to the class.

- Students working in groups are more active than if they're working as a class: they talk more and do more thinking too. If a class of, say, twenty were doing an eight-question exercise 'round the class' most of them wouldn't answer a single question.

- If an exercise is done 'round the class', the lazier students can simply answer 'I don't know' when their turn comes and go to sleep the rest of the time. The weaker students can be lulled into a false sense of security by writing down all the correct answers and convincing themselves that they have 'done' the exercise.

The drawback of doing exercises in pairs or groups is that it does take time. However, as many of the exercises can be done as homework, time can be saved by setting some exercises to be done at home. Then, back in class next time, students can begin the session by comparing their answers in pairs or groups and discussing as a class any problems they encountered.

'My students talk in their own language when they're in pairs.'

How can students be discouraged from using their native language – and encouraged to speak only in English?

While using *Making Progress*, students will be participating in enjoyable speaking activities. The problem is that their enjoyment (and desire to express their ideas) may tempt them to lapse into their native language from time to time. When this happens, you might find it helpful to remind them that every member of the class has a common aim: to improve his or her English. Indeed, one of the guiding principles of *Making Progress* is to foster a spirit of cooperation and friendship in the class and to give students the feeling that they all have a role to play in the success of the course. Agree together on this rule: 'Only English may be spoken in our class.' That may sound like a tall order, but it's something everyone should aim for.

Here are some ideas that may help if your students are finding it difficult to follow the English-only rule:

- Remind them that your class is their only opportunity to use English during the week.
- Go round monitoring and, whenever you overhear a pair or group speaking their mother tongue, remind them firmly of the 'English-only' rule.
- Introduce a light-hearted system of 'fines' (rather like a swear box) for students who don't use English. (Use the proceeds for a party at the end of the year, perhaps. Or to buy a class dictionary.)
- Before the students are split into pairs or groups, demonstrate what they have to do. Use one of your more confident students as your own partner while the others listen. This will help everyone to get into the discussion or role play more quickly.
- Separate students who persistently use their own language together. Put them with students who do use English in class – but not if they have a bad influence on anyone they sit with. Sometimes students working in a group of three are less likely to lapse into their mother tongue than students in pairs. (So feel free to interpret 👥👥 as 👥👥👥 from time to time!)
- Make sure everyone knows the simple 'classroom language' they can use to manage their interaction. Quite often these phrases come so naturally in their own language that it's difficult to break the habit. To help everyone to learn and remember, make a list of phrases like these on the board (or put them on a poster for the classroom):

I'm sorry, I don't understand what we have to do.
Can you repeat the instructions please?
Who's going to begin?
You begin.
I'll begin, OK?
Whose turn is it?
What are we supposed to do?
How long do we have to do this?

I didn't hear what you said.
What does this word mean?
Let's ask the teacher about this.
I think we've finished. What should we do now?

Could you repeat that, please?
Could you speak more slowly, please?
Could I borrow a pen/pencil, etc., please?
Can you lend me a pen/pencil, please?

What does 'fierce' mean?
How do you say . . . in English?
How do you spell 'castle'?
How do you pronounce this word?
What's the past tense/past participle of 'lie'?
Can you give me an example?
Could you say that again, please?

– and add further similar phrases to the list or poster as the need arises.

'What should I do when my students make mistakes?'

Although most learners using *Making Progress* should already have a basic knowledge of English grammar, they will still make plenty of mistakes. Accuracy is an important aspect of language learning and should never be ignored, but it's more important for students to be able to communicate effectively. Many grammatical mistakes don't seriously affect communication. No student should be corrected every time he or she makes a mistake. If that happened, many students would become inhibited and afraid to speak at all! Actually, mistakes are an essential indicator of what still needs to be learnt. On the basis of the mistakes you overhear, together with the types of questions students ask you, you can plan any additional practice your class may require.

Students should certainly be corrected when they make serious errors which impede communication or lead to misunderstandings. However, it's usually best to point out any mistakes that were made after everyone has completed an activity, rather than interrupting during the activity. While students are working in pairs or groups and you're going from group to group, you might be able to make the occasional discreet correction without interrupting the flow of the conversation. It's usually better, however, to make a note of some of the errors you overhear and point them out later.

When making a note of errors, use a proper notebook, not scrap paper, so that you can keep a permanent record of what your class is doing. This will also help you to see the progress they're making and detect what kinds of mistakes are the most persistent. Using a proper notebook also shows the class that you're taking this aspect of the lesson seriously, and not having a rest while they do the work! The purpose of all this is to make it clear to the class that they can learn from their mistakes.

Rather than randomly noting down every mistake you hear, it's a good idea to focus systematically on different kinds of mistakes in different lessons: today 'prepositions', next time 'past tenses', next time 'pronunciation', and so on. Then the feedback you give the class can be helpful and systematic, rather than confusing or even demoralizing. This will help them to focus on improving different problems, one at a time. If you've decided to focus on, say, 'prepositions' and today you only hear a couple of mistakes, let the class know and congratulate them accordingly!

For advice on correcting mistakes in writing see page 14.

Vocabulary

It's important to limit the definition of vocabulary to those words that are essential to the task. Students can often complete an activity successfully without understanding every word. In fact, students should be encouraged to develop a tolerance for ambiguity so they don't panic when they see an unfamiliar word. By focusing on essential vocabulary only, you can use their time in class more efficiently.

Before you explain the meaning of a word, ask students if they can explain its meaning. If no one can, encourage students to guess the meaning of a word from its context – an important reading and listening skill. At first, students may need your guidance, but as their skill develops, they will be able to do this on their own. Explain that guessing the meaning of a word from its context involves:

- looking at the other words in the sentence for clues
- thinking about what they know about similar words
- using their knowledge of the world
- thinking of similar words in their own language

Students are more likely to remember the new words if they work out meanings for themselves, than if you define the word for them in English or translate it into their own language.

Students may find highlighting new words is a useful aid to remembering them. Besides highlighting, students should be encouraged to store vocabulary in other ways: a loose-leaf personal organizer or Filofax is particularly useful for this. This can best be done by topics, with each new topic starting on a new page. Fresh pages can be inserted whenever necessary and the pages and topics can be rearranged easily. Some students may prefer to do this electronically using a laptop.

Listening

Listening is a skill that requires the students to concentrate on what they do understand and not to worry about all the things they don't understand. If a speaker says something unclearly, there's no point in worrying about this if it means that you stop listening to what he or she says next. In real life we have to ignore the words we don't understand and concentrate on the main points that are being made. It would be impossible for the students to acquire this skill if the only English that they were exposed to was always slow and simple. Using the recordings in *Making Progress* will help the students to do this better. The tasks in the book help students to understand the main points the speakers make.

Try to 'set the scene' for students before they hear the recording by explaining where the speakers are and what their relationship is (colleagues, good friends, strangers, or whatever). In class students will be trying to understand disembodied voices coming out of a loudspeaker and this is much more difficult than being in the same room as a real person who is speaking. In some **Listening** exercises there are photos of the speakers to help students to empathize with them a little.

Most classes will need to hear each recording at least twice to extract all the required information. In some cases, where a class are weak at listening, you may need to pause the tape frequently and replay certain sections to help them to understand more easily. However, it's essential for students to realize that they don't have to be able to understand every single word to answer the questions in class – or in real life.

Here's a recommended procedure for the **Listening** exercises:

1 Before the lesson, look at the transcript and, if possible, listen to the recording. Try to anticipate the difficulties your class may have. Highlight any words or expressions you want to explain to them before you play the recording. Decide where you will pause a longer recording and mark the places in pencil on your transcript.

2 In class, explain what the recording is about, how many speakers there are, who they are and where they are. In some **Listening** sections there are some warm-up discussion questions to do before the actual listening.

3 Ask everyone to read the questions or the task before you play the recording.

4 Set the counter to zero if using a cassette player. If using a CD player make a note of the track number.

5 Play the recording all the way through so that students can imagine the situations, get used to the voices and get the gist of what is being said. (If the recording is too long for this, just play the first 15–20 seconds, then rewind to zero – or back to the beginning of the track.)

6 Play the recording again and this time ask everyone to decide on their answers to the questions in the **Student's Book**.

7 Get everyone to compare their answers. If they haven't managed to answer all the questions, they may need to hear it again.

8 If necessary, play the recording again so that everyone has another attempt at getting the answers they missed before.

9 Finally, play the recording for a third time and ask them to just sit back and listen. Maybe they could note down any questions they want to ask you at the end, or note down vocabulary or expressions that were used – or just relax and enjoy the conversations while soaking up ideas and vocabulary. (This would be a good time for the students to look at the transcript if they're using the **Self-study Student's Book**.)

10 Encourage students to share their reactions to the content with each other and talk more about the topic. In many **Listening** sections there are follow-up discussion questions.

Reading

It's essential for students to realize that they don't have to be able to understand every single word to answer the questions in class – or in the exam. They should concentrate on what the writers are trying to say and the information they're communicating. Unfamiliar words in a **Reading** text may be distracting but students shouldn't assume that they're all important and 'worth learning'.

Before they attempt the comprehension task for a text ask the class to decide:

*   what the text is about
*   who wrote it
*   who the intended readers are
*   where they think it's taken from

Then they should skim the text (read it through very rapidly to get an idea of what it's about and what the main points are). Then they should read it through more carefully and answer the questions.

Writing

When marking students' written work, you can't really overlook some of their mistakes as you would do when they're talking. However, it's helpful to show students which of their mistakes are more serious and which less serious, and to distinguish between different kinds of mistakes.

When your students submit written work to you, ask them to leave a wide margin so that there's plenty of room for you to add comments later. If there's a better way of saying something or a better word to use, you may want to write that in as a suggestion.

When marking students' written work, don't forget how discouraging it is to receive back a paper covered in red marks! It's better for students to locate and correct their own mistakes, rather than have corrections written out for them. This is particularly important when you believe that a student has made a careless mistake or a slip of the pen. Often, once mistakes are pointed out to students, they can correct them themselves.

And don't only highlight mistakes: it's important to give encouragement in equal measure. A tick (✓) is a nice way of showing that an idea has been well expressed. Words of encouragement are even more appreciated – especially if a student seems to have put a lot of effort into his or her work.

A marking scheme like the one below is recommended – but whatever scheme you do use make sure your students are conversant with the system. The symbols shown here would appear on the side of the page in the margin – make sure your students do leave a margin, therefore!

✗ = 'Somewhere in this line there's a mistake of some kind that you should find and correct'

✗ ✗ = 'Somewhere in this line there are two mistakes that you should find and correct'

An <u>inncorect</u> word or phrase underlined

◯ = 'This particular word or phrase isn't correct and you should correct it'

G = 'Somewhere in this line there's a grammatical mistake that you should find and correct'

V = 'Somewhere in this line there's a vocabulary mistake that you should find and correct'

Sp = 'Somewhere in this line there's a spelling mistake that you should find and correct'

P = 'Somewhere in this line there's a punctuation mistake that you should find and correct'

WO = 'Some of the words in this sentence aren't in the correct word order so please rearrange them'

? = 'I don't quite understand what you mean'

And equally important:

✓ = 'Good, you've expressed this idea well!' or 'This is an interesting or amusing point!'

✓✓ = 'Very good, you've expressed this idea very well!' or 'Very interesting or amusing point!'

Remember that all learners need encouragement and praise. Just as you might sometimes ignore mistakes when students are speaking, perhaps occasionally some mistakes should be overlooked in their written work?

Acknowledgements

The author and publishers are grateful to HarperCollins Children's Books for permission to use the extract on p. 135 from *A Series of Unfortunate Events: The Bad Beginning*, by Lemony Snicket.

The FCE exam

The Cambridge ESOL (English for Speakers of Other Languages) FCE (First Certificate in English) exam is held in June and in December each year. The exam assesses general proficiency in English through the testing of the candidates' abilities in reading, writing, speaking and listening and their knowledge of vocabulary and grammar.

PAPER 1: READING *1 hour 15 minutes*

Part	Task type	Focus	Number of questions	Task format
1	Multiple matching	Understanding the gist, the main points, detail, the structure of the text, specific information, or deducing the meaning	6–7	A text preceded by multiple matching questions. Candidates have to match an item from one list with an item from another list, or match items to elements within the text itself.
2	Multiple choice	As Part 1	7–8	A text followed by four-option multiple choice questions.
3	Gapped text	Understanding the gist, the main points, detail and text structure	6–7	A text from which paragraphs or sentences have been removed followed by the removed items in jumbled order. Candidates have to decide where in the text the items were removed from.
4	Multiple matching or multiple choice	As Part 1	13–15	as Part 1

- One part may contain one text, or two or more shorter texts.
- The texts may come from any of these sources: advertisements, correspondence, fiction, brochures, guide books, manuals, messages, newspaper articles, magazine articles or reports.
- In all, candidates have to read 1,900–2,300 words (about 350–700 words per text).
- Candidates indicate their answers by shading the correct lozenges on the special answer sheet. The total number of marks is 40 (20% of the total).

PAPER 2: WRITING *1 hour 30 minutes*

Part	Task type and focus	Number of tasks and length	Task format
1	Question 1 Writing a transactional letter	1 compulsory task 120–180 words	The candidate is guided by 1–3 short texts and sometimes visual prompts as well as by the rubric (instructions).
2	Questions 2–4 Writing one of the following: an article; an informal or non-transactional letter; a discursive composition; a descriptive or narrative composition or short story	4 tasks from which candidates choose 1 120–180 words	The task or composition is explained in the rubric.
	Question 5 Writing one of the above on a prescribed background reading text	2 options	The task is explained in the rubric.

- Part 1 (Question 1) is compulsory.
- For Part 2, candidates choose ONE question from Questions 2–5.
- Candidates may be asked to write any of the following task types: letters, articles, reports, compositions or essays – all written for a given purpose and target reader.
- Candidates write in a special answer booklet which is read and marked by an examiner. The total number of marks is 40 (20% of the total).
- The examiners have followed standardized induction, training and coordination procedures and use criterion-referenced assessment scales. The scales assess such language features as: range of vocabulary and structure; accuracy of vocabulary, structures, spelling and punctuation; appropriacy; organization and cohesion; task achievement.

PAPER 3: USE OF ENGLISH *1 hour 15 minutes*

Part	Task type	Focus	Number of questions	Task format
1	Multiple choice cloze	Emphasis on vocabulary	15	A 'modified cloze' text with 15 gaps, followed by 15 four-option multiple choice questions.
2	Open cloze	Grammar and vocabulary	15	A 'modified cloze' text with 15 gaps.
3	Key word transformations	Grammar and vocabulary	10	Sentences with gaps. The gaps must be filled using the given word and other words which are necessary, but without changing the meaning of the sentence.

PAPER 3: USE OF ENGLISH *Continued*

Part	Task type	Focus	Number of questions	Task format
4	Error correction	Emphasis on grammar	15	A text containing errors. Some lines are correct, some lines contain an extra unnecessary word which must be identified.
5	Word formation	Vocabulary	10	A text with 10 gaps. Each gap must be filled with a word formed from the 'stem' word which is given beside the text.

- Candidates write their answers on the special answer sheet.
  The total number of marks is 65, which is 'scaled down' to 40 (20% of the total).

PAPER 4: LISTENING *40 minutes approximately*

Part	Task type	Focus	Number of questions	Task format
1	Multiple choice	Understanding gist, main points, function, location, roles and relationships, mood, attitude, intention, feeling or opinion	8	A series of short unrelated extracts (about 30 seconds each) from monologues or interacting speakers. The multiple choice questions have three options.
2	Note taking or blank filling	Understanding gist, main points, detail or specific information, or deducing meaning	10	A monologue or interacting speakers (about 3 minutes).
3	Multiple matching	As Part 1	5	A series of short related extracts (about 30 seconds each) from monologues or interacting speakers. In the multiple matching questions candidates have to select the correct items from a list.
4	Selection from 2 or 3 possible answers	As Part 2	7	A monologue or interacting speakers (about 3 minutes). Candidates have to select between 2 or 3 possible answers: *True/False*, *Yes/No*, three-option multiple choice, which speaker said what, etc.

- Each text is heard twice.
- The recordings contain a variety of accents.
- The monologues may include the following text types: answerphone messages, commentaries, documentaries, instructions, lectures, news, public announcements, advertisements, reports, speeches, talks, stories or anecdotes.

- The interacting speakers may be taking part in: chats, conversations, discussions, interviews, quizzes, radio drama or transactions.
- Candidates indicate their answers by shading the correct lozenges or by writing the correct word or words on the special answer sheet. The total number of marks is 30, which is 'scaled up' to 40 (20% of the total).

PAPER 5: SPEAKING *14 minutes approximately*

Part	Task type	Focus	Length	Task format
1	Short exchanges between each candidate and the interlocutor	Giving personal information and socializing	3 minutes	The candidates give personal information about themselves.
2	Long turn from each candidate with brief response from the other candidate	Exchanging personal and factual information, expressing attitudes and opinions, using discourse functions related to managing a long turn	4 minutes	The candidates are in turn given two colour photographs. They each talk about their photographs for about a minute. They are also asked to comment briefly on each other's photographs.
3	Candidates talk with each other	Exchanging information, expressing attitudes and opinions	3 minutes	The candidates are given visual prompts (photographs, line drawings, diagrams, etc.) which generate a discussion while they take part in tasks such as planning, problem solving, decision making, prioritizing, speculating, etc.
4	Candidates talk with each other and with the interlocutor	Exchanging and justifying opinions	4 minutes	The interlocutor encourages the candidates to discuss other aspects of the topic of Part 3.

- Parts 2–4 are based on the same general theme.
- There are usually two candidates together with two examiners. One examiner acts mainly as interlocutor and manages the interaction by asking questions or giving the candidates cues. The other acts as assessor and does not join in the conversation.
- The examiners have followed standardized induction, training and coordination procedures and use criterion-referenced assessment scales. The scales assess such language features as: use of grammar; use of vocabulary; pronunciation; interactive communication and task achievement.
- This paper contributes 20% of the total marks.

RESULTS

Candidates are given semi-profiled results on their result slips. These show them in which particular papers their performance was very good or very weak. Pass certificates are issued to candidates who gain grades A, B or C. Certificates are not issued to candidates with failing grades: D, E or U (unclassified).

1 Personal information

1A You and me
1B Family and friends

The aims of **1A** and **1B** are:

- to encourage students to work together in pairs and to appreciate the benefits and pleasures of working with a partner
- to help all the members of the class to get to know each other better
- to encourage everyone to talk about their likes and dislikes, families and personalities
- to revise the use of present simple and past simple
- to practise saying different numbers and figures
- to practise writing a short, friendly e-mail

Experience is the name every one gives to their mistakes.
A friend is one who knows all about you and likes you anyway. – Christi Mary Warner
How rare and wonderful is that flash of a moment when we realize we have discovered a friend. – William Rotsler
Friendship is like money, easier made than kept. – Samuel Butler
A true friend is one who overlooks your failures and tolerates your success. – Doug Larson

---

1A You and me

What sort of person are you?

Speaking and vocabulary

1 Arrange the class into an EVEN number of pairs, so that they can be combined into groups in **3** later. To achieve this with an odd number of students, some 'pairs' may need to be groups of three. This kind of discussion will work just as well in threes.

➡ Whenever the symbol 👥 appears in the Student's Book, groups of three may be more effective, especially with students who lack confidence. In any case, whenever there is an odd number of students, one 'pair' will have to be a group of three.

The speech balloon shows how the conversations might go. If necessary, demonstrate this with one of your more confident students, continuing the conversation about a few more of the mis-coloured pictures:

What about this taxi? It's supposed to be a New York taxi, isn't it?
— Yes. But it's the wrong colour.
What colour should it be?
— Well, if it's a New York taxi, it shouldn't be red.
— No that's right. What colour should it be?
— It should be yellow.
Yes of course. How about this next picture?

Suggested answers

If it's a New York taxi, it shouldn't be red, it should be yellow.
If it's the sky, it shouldn't be green, it should be blue.
If it's a penguin, it shouldn't be pink, it should be black and white.
If it's a leaf, it shouldn't be grey, it should be green.
If it's an orange, it shouldn't be purple, it should be orange.

For the second part students can use dictionaries if they don't know some of the colours. Point out that the first letter of each colour is given as a clue! Alternatively this could be done by brainstorming as a whole class. Check the spelling of the colours.

Answers

aqua   beige   magenta   olive   plum   teal   turquoise

2 ◀ Although, obviously, students will be listening 'alone' to the recording, keep them in pairs so that they can do it 'together' – helping each other with the task and checking each other's answers after each listening.

⟹ If your students have little experience of listening to real English speakers, this may be quite hard at first – it's difficult to catch every word they say, just as in real life. However, the task makes it much easier and it should only take two or three goes to get all the information. Often students panic when hearing unfamiliar voices for the first time. You can help them to feel more secure by playing the first 20 seconds of the recording to them to let them get accustomed to the voices, then rewind and ask them to do the task.

👥 The follow-up to the listening requires the pairs to talk about their own preferences, having the same sort of conversation they've just heard. Maybe play Anna and Max again as a model before they start.

Quickly make sure everyone knows the colours illustrated are:

black   blue   brown   green   pink   purple   red   white   yellow   grey

Answers

Anna likes	(dark) blue, red, yellow, grey and purple
She doesn't like	green or pink
Max likes	green, blue and red
He doesn't like	yellow, grey, pink and purple

Transcript 1 minute 40 seconds (with answers in **bold** type)

Presenter: Anna is with her friend Max. She's reading a magazine article about colours and how they can reflect your personality. Listen.

Anna: What's your favourite colour, Max?

Max: Um…er…favourite colour? Er…never really thought about it. Um…I don't know…er…green, I think I like **green** the best. Um…why…why do you want to know?

Anna: Well, it says here in this magazine article: 'What sort of person are you?' It says that colours you like reflect your personality.

Max: Really?

Anna: Mm!

Max: Oh! What about you, then? What's your favourite colour?

Anna: Well, I like **blue**, w…dark blue particularly.

Max: Mm . . . Well, I like **blue** as well. Yeah, blue's a really good colour.

Anna: Mm.

Max: Any other favourites? What else do you like?

Anna: Er…well, I'm not really keen on **green**, but…um…ah, **red** is nice.

Max: Yeah.

Anna: Yeah, oh and **yellow**.

Max: Yellow? You like yellow? Oh, I really hate **yellow**. Do you know what I really hate, though? **Grey**. Do you?

Anna: Oh no! I think grey's OK. I really like **grey**. Ah, how about…how about **pink**, what do you think of pink?

Max: No, I don't like **pink**!

Anna:	Haha!
Max:	Do you?
Anna:	No, not really. Yeah, but **purple**. Now purple's a really strong colour.
Max:	Yeah, but I don't like that. **Purple!**
Anna:	Yeah!
Max:	Horrible.
Anna:	Haha!
Max:	Can you see me in purple?
Anna:	Oh, definitely.

3 👥+👥 Combine the pairs as they look at Communication **Activity 1** on page 131. This is part of the magazine article that Anna was reading. Encourage everyone to discuss what they read and be as sceptical as they like! Tell them how long they have for this – two minutes should be enough.

> With any kind of pair or group discussion it's essential to inform the students how long is available for the discussion. If you don't do this, they won't be able to pace themselves and make the most of the time they have. If they don't know how long they have, students tend to rush through the questions or task for fear of not finishing – and do the activity as quickly as possible.

Doing this together in pairs is more fun and will encourage the students to interact. Change the pairs around so that everyone has a new partner to speak to for this part – this will help everyone to get to know each other better.

4 🔊 Play the recording once only. But if everyone is finding this difficult, stop after a minute or so, rewind and then start again. This will allow everyone time to have got used to Claire's voice. It shouldn't be necessary to pause the recording while it's playing because Claire gives her listeners time to do their drawings. Make sure everyone has a clean sheet of paper (at least A5 but preferably A4) and a pencil ready.

👥 The continuation of the recording shows everyone what they might say when they look at **Activity 21** on page 136. If possible let the recording continue playing to lead everyone into this activity.

Transcript 3 minutes 30 seconds

Presenter:	Listen to Claire. She's going to give some instructions to Jill and James. Follow her instructions and do exactly what she says. You'll need a clean sheet of paper for this.
Claire:	OK, everyone. First of all, um…get a piece of paper and a pen or pencil. . . . Yeah? Everyone sorted?
Others:	Yes. Yep.
Claire:	OK. I would like you to draw the outline of a house. . . . yep . . . Whatever house you want. . . . That's it. Just the outline. . . . Ready?
Others:	Uh-huh.
Claire:	Now draw the front door. . . . Don't think about it, just draw the front door. . . . And when you're done with that, you can add any windows you want. . . . As many as you like. Yeah. Good. . . . Fine. . . . Now I want you to draw an arrow where you'd like your bedroom to be. . . . It can be any one of these rooms, is the one where you sleep. . . . That's a big arrow. . . . And when you're finished with that, you can draw your garden. . . . That's it trees, flowers, whatever you think is in your garden. . . . That's great. . . . OK? And now draw a picture of yourself next to the house. . . . And when you're finished, you need to look at Activity 21 to find out how to interpret your drawing. . . .

James:	Right, so Activity 21. Let's see what it says our pictures say about our personalities. . . . Um…it says: 'If your house is made up of clear thick lines, you are a strong leader'. Right. Well, I think we know who the strong leader is . . .
Jill:	Hooray!
James:	. . . in this group. Very nice. Um…and then: 'It's got…if your house is made up of wavy, thin lines, you are often indecisive.' . . . Do you think they're wavy and thin?
Jill:	A bit wavy, a bit.
James:	They might be a bit thin. OK…um… 'If your door is detailed, your life is orderly and predictable.'
Jill:	Mine is.
James:	Yours is quite…you've got a lot of detail there . . .
Jill:	. . . not that orderly and predictable . . .
James:	That's obviously wrong. 'If your door has no details, your life is often full of changes.'
Jill:	Oh, interesting . . .

5 👥 Change the pairs around again for this. Students will need to use dictionaries to look up any unfamiliar words. Tell everyone how much time they have for this – at least three minutes.

At the end
Combine the pairs into groups for them to compare their decisions.

Extra questions for discussion
- Which adjectives do NOT describe your personalities well?
- Can you think of any other adjectives that describe your personalities just as well, or better?

This section focuses on irregular verbs, as well as the formation of the present simple and the past simple, and the use of *do/does* and *did*.

Present simple and past simple

Grammar practice

Typical mistakes
She feeled unwell.
She is driving her car to work every day.
What you did on holiday?

and incorrect irregular verb forms

1 If at all possible, ask everyone to prepare for this section by looking at the Grammar reference section before the lesson. If they can't manage to do this, allow everyone time to read it before beginning **2**.

⟹ The Grammar reference sections on pages 118 to 130 are an integral part of the Student's Book. Each section relates directly to the grammar points covered in the Grammar practice exercises, providing helpful examples and relevant rules of use. As studying these sections is best done at students' own pace, encourage everyone to study these sections before the lesson.

If this is not possible, a few minutes' silent study may make a nice change of pace in a lively lesson with lots of interaction.

2 This exercise gives everyone a chance to find out what they know, or don't know.

Answers

1 went   didn't fall
2 boils   freezes   fell *or* was   froze   heat   becomes/turns into
3 goes/comes   went/came

3 👥 Doing this in pairs encourages everyone to discuss alternatives and consider which answers are best – and come up with interesting or amusing answers.

Suggested answers

1 have coffee*   had tea   did/do you have
2 feel upset/angry   feel happy/pleased   feel grateful (*or* am upset, etc.)
3 felt upset   felt happy   felt grateful (*or* was upset, etc.)

* There are many possible variations: stay at home, have cereal, don't have anything, don't eat anything, etc.

4 👥👥 Tell everyone how long they have for this, so that they don't rush through the questions. They should ask each other for details. Allow four or five minutes.

At the end

Recombine the class and ask various students some of these extra questions:

- When do you usually have your meals?
- What do you like to eat?
- Where did you go for your last holiday?
- What did you do on holiday?

Correct any mistakes in using verbs.

Numbers

Pronunciation and vocabulary

This section focuses on saying numbers clearly (so that they can be understood), and understanding numbers when they are spoken aloud.

➡ Numbers are surprisingly difficult for learners. This is probably because they translate all numbers into their own language before processing them. Everyone needs to understand phone numbers and prices, which are terribly hard to understand in a foreign language and with foreign currency.

1 👥 Besides recognizing where these numbers might be seen, ask everyone to say them aloud too.

Suggested answers (o is pronounced / əʊ /)

phone number – plus four four (forty-four), one, two, O* two, double four, double two, five, six
time – eleven fifty-three
credit card – nine nine two O, O two two four, O four nine one, three O four
passport number – seven O, double two, one nine, two eight O
radio frequency – ninety-eight point one
number on calculator – zero[†] point seven seven three four

* O can be *zero* in all these examples
[†] *zero* can be *nought* here

2 🔊 👥 Pause the recording after each line to give everyone time to finish writing. At the end the pairs should compare answers. Then play the recording again for everyone to get the ones they missed or were unsure of. Finally, the students take turns to say the sentences aloud.

Transcript and Answers 2 minutes 10 seconds

Presenter: Fill the gaps in each sentence with the numbers you hear.

1	My telephone number is three eight four three double nine.	**384399**
	The Moon is three hundred and eighty-four thousand, three hundred and ninety-nine kilometres from the Earth.	**384,399**
2	My passport number is one O nine two four.	**10924**
	The deepest part of the Pacific Ocean is ten thousand, nine hundred and twenty-four metres deep.	**10,924**
3	Their car registration number is JG eight, eight, four, eight.	**8848**
	The height of Mount Everest is eight thousand, eight hundred and forty-eight metres.	**8,848**
4	The price of this CD is fourteen pounds ninety-nine.	**14.99**
	Seventy-four point nine five divided by five equals fourteen point nine nine.	**14.99**
5	One and a quarter multiplied by three is three and three-quarters.	**3¾**
	Five times nought point seven five is three point seven five.	**3.75**

3 👥 Point out the Advice Box to everyone. Perhaps start everyone off by dictating one number of each type of your own choosing to the class.

At the end
Ask members of the class to dictate their 'important number' to everyone else. Who can guess what that number refers to?

1B Family and friends

Just relax

Listening

1 👥 Tell everyone how long they have for this discussion – three minutes is about right.

2 🔊 This begins as a reading task, before becoming a listening task. Allow everyone time to read the 13 pieces of advice before they hear the recording. Reading the advice will make it much easier to understand the recording.

You'll probably need to play the recording at least twice. Between listenings, encourage the pairs to compare answers.

Answers
The only points they did NOT mention were: 4, 9 and 13.

Transcript 2 minutes 30 seconds

Presenter: You're going to hear a radio programme. Martha is interviewing the authors of a new book about avoiding stress. Listen to the programme and tick the advice that the speakers give.

Martha (presenter): Now, stress is something that most of us suffer from. Tim Radford and Jenny Harris have just published a book: *500 Ways To Avoid Stress*. So, out of those five hundred, Tim, what's your best tip of all?

Tim: Ha! Well, it's…it's quite hard to pick…er…just one, Martha. But…er…what I would say is, quite simply: **one minute of laughter is as reviving as doing a good forty-five minutes of exercise**. It really is.

Martha: Oh, OK. Jenny?

Jenny: Um…well, er…i…if you don't have a pet, borrow one, because…er…**ten minutes stroking an animal will reduce your blood pressure**, just ten minutes.

Tim: Yeah, and that's very true, er…and another thing you can do is make a list – lists are good – **make a list of ten things that make you happy** and…and try and incorporate them…build them in to…to your daily life.

Jenny: And of course, the old favourite: **Um…eating little and often…er…that helps keep blood sugar levels up**.

Tim: Mhm, mhm. Um…and also, **walking**. Walking is superb, it's such a relaxing form of exercise and whilst you're doing it, it really does give you a chance to think.

Jenny: Absolutely, yeah. Um…er…**take twenty deep breaths ten times a day**. Er…that balances and replenishes the body and mind.

Tim: Mhm, mhm. And on…on body and mind in particular: a **good posture**, a really good posture, i…it actually means your body is feeling…it…it's not feeling those…those effects that you get when you feel tense. You know, those…those . . .

Jenny: All seized up?

Tim: Yeah, just by moderating your posture: walking tall. That really does the job.

Jenny: **Have a haircut!** I…I mean . . .

Martha and Tim: Haha!

Jenny: But, you know, I mean it's a quick way to feel, and look, better.

Martha: I'm in favour of that. Just one more from you each, we're running out of time.

Tim: OK, well, what I'd say is: **don't be afraid of spending…um…time on your own**. Time alone is very important because it…it allows you to take stock of what's been going on that day.

Jenny: And also, of course, just like tonight: um…spend time with a friend. You know, make dinner, have a good chat. Just…just relax in one another's company.

Tim: Yeah.

Martha: Jenny and Tim, thanks very much.

Jenny and Tim: Thank you.

3 👥👥 Tell everyone how long they have for this discussion. Allow a good five minutes so that they can develop their ideas and justify their views.

At the end
Ask the class to tell the others about their other ideas for helping each other to relax.

(More tips in the Workbook)

Writing to a friend

1 👥 There are no fixed rules about composing e-mails, especially to friends. But a friend will be surprised if you write in a formal style. An e-mail is rather like a conversation without the pauses and hesitations.

Ask everyone to look at the e-mail together, imagining it came from their friend (who could be female or male, as they prefer).

2 👥 The same pairs decide how they will answer Alex's questions. Encourage them to think what questions they can ask Alex him/herself.

3 ✎ This is a short task, which could be done in class. Or you may prefer to set this as homework.

The Model version is not, of course, the 'correct answer'. It is just a model to show to students.

Model version

Dear Alex,

Great to hear from you after so long! I'm really sorry I haven't been in touch but I've been pretty busy.

We are all well and my little sister has just started primary school and comes home every day full of stories about her adventures!

Yes, I'm still studying English. We've just started a new course and we're using a new book which makes learning really fun! I'm still with the same friends in class as before so that's nice too. Our new teacher is really kind and helpful.

I had a wonderful holiday – it seems so long ago now! We drove all round the island, stopping at different villages and beaches. We stayed in an old farmhouse with fields all around. The weather was pretty good, apart from one day with a spectacular thunderstorm!

How about you? What is your news?

How are you all?

What was your holiday like?

We really must keep in touch. I'll write again soon.

Very best wishes,

Kim

© Cambridge University Press, 2005

4 👥 Students read their partner's e-mail and write a short reply to it. Then they reply to the reply! (If this is going to take too long in class, some of the writing can be done as homework.)

Likes and dislikes

Speaking

1 🔊 This section begins with pronunciation practice. Play the recording. There is a pause after each line for everyone to repeat the sentence. Do this a few times until everyone feels comfortable with the phrases and can say them easily and confidently.

Transcript 1 minutes 20 seconds

Man:	What is your favourite colour?
Woman:	Well, I do like blue but I think I like red more.
Man:	Do you like pink?
Woman	I don't really have a favourite, but I do like yellow a lot.
Man:	Why do you like yellow so much?
Woman:	Because it reminds me of sunshine.
Man:	What colour do you dislike most?
1st Woman:	That's hard to say, but I don't like grey very much.
Man:	Why don't you like grey?

| 1st Woman: | I'm not sure really. |
| 2nd Woman: | What about you? What's your favourite . . . ? |

2 👥 Arrange the class into an even number of pairs for this. Encourage everyone to use the phrases as they interview their partner and complete the chart with the partner's favourites. Make sure everyone knows how long they have for this – allow a good five minutes.

3 👥+👥 Combine the pairs into groups for them to compare their tastes.

At the end
Reassemble the class and find out whether there are any top favourites and 'unfavourites' in each category.

2 Learning English

2A The English language
2B A better memory?

The aims of **2A** and **2B** are:

*   to increase students' awareness of the English language and to use the necessary terminology to refer to different kinds of words and structures
*   to encourage students to use dictionaries intelligently
*   to foster different ways of storing and memorizing new vocabulary
*   to revise the use of prepositions
*   to revise punctuation

There are hundreds of languages in the world, but a smile speaks them all.
A retentive memory may be a good thing, but the ability to forget is the true token of greatness.
A smile happens in a flash, but its memory can last a lifetime.

2A The English language

Talking about language and communication

Speaking and vocabulary

1 👥 Allow everyone three or four minutes for this, maybe combining the pairs into groups after two minutes. Encourage everyone to think of more examples of the possible pitfalls of relying on phrase-books and dictionaries:

*   The way you say something (your tone of voice) may be misinterpreted
*   Saying a string of words you don't understand may be risky
*   You probably won't be able to understand the answer someone gives you
*   You may choose a word with a completely different meaning from the one you intend
*   Some words have several meanings: teddy *bear*, I can't *bear* the pain, *bear* left, to *bear* a child – not to mention *bare* = naked! etc.

2 👥 This is best done as a discussion in pairs, with everyone solving the 'puzzle' together. Allow a little time for discussion at the end. Deal with questions arising, before going through all the correct answers.

Answers [in square brackets]

Mrs Duncan had done her shopping at the **[noun]**. She **[phrasal verb]** to her car in the car park, and found four **[adjective]** men in the car. She screamed **[preposition]** them **[phrase]**, 'Get out of the car! I have a gun and I know how to use it!' The four men jumped out of the car and ran like mad. She **[verb]** her shopping bags into **[article]** back of the car and got into the driver's seat. But her key wouldn't fit the ignition. This was when she realized that this **[modal verb]** be her car. *[italics]* car was parked in the next row. She put her stuff **[preposition]** her own car and drove **[adverb]** to the police station. She felt guilty and wanted to explain her terrible mistake.

[sentence] He pointed to the other end of the counter where four pale young men had just reported that a mad woman had stolen their car.

[paragraph]

3 👥 Doing this in pairs helps everyone to feel more confident and to pool their knowledge. Other variants may be possible, so allow time to discuss these if necessary.

Answers

1	vowels	2	alphabet consonants	3	translate examples
4	accents (or dialects)	5	expresssion/face	6	gesture/sign

4 👥👥 After the group discussion, reassemble the class and ask for a brief report from some groups.

Find out how many people speak your students' language(s), in case they don't know. Here are some figures:

Top ten native speakers

1	Chinese	1,000	million
2	English	350	
3	Spanish	250	
4	Hindi	200	
5	Arabic	150	
6	Bengali	150	
7	Russian	150	
8	Portuguese	135	
9	Japanese	120	
10	German	100	

Prepositions – 1
Grammar practice

➡ Prepositions are only little words (or phrases), but they are a big problem area for most students. At this level they already know how to use prepositions in plenty of ways, but there are still areas of doubt and contexts where they may make mistakes. It may be best to reassure them how much they do already know, rather than focus on mistakes. Only rarely does an incorrect preposition cause a misunderstanding.

Typical mistakes

He was sitting before the fire.
It's on left of the house.
He walked away the house.
She came out the building.
He came by the train.
What happened on the end?
He never arrives at time.

1 The Grammar reference section on page 119 summarizes some of the main uses of prepositions in general. Students should study this **before** the lesson, if possible.

You may prefer to get the students to try **2** first to see how they get on and to test themselves on what they already know. Then, perhaps, refer them to the Grammar reference section to help them sort out any problems.

2 👥 **Answers**

Four American bank managers flew **to** Australia to take part **in** a golf tournament. They all had bright green jackets **with** the name **of** their bank **in** large letters **on** the back. **After** the tournament they had a day free, so they decided to rent a car and drive **out of** the city. They drove **into** the country, hoping to see some kangaroos.

But they were **out of** luck. **After** driving **for** hours, they didn't see a single kangaroo. So they turned the car around and started to drive back **to** the city. **At** that very moment a kangaroo hopped **into** the road directly **in** front **of** them, and they hit the poor animal. It landed **with** a thud **in/on** the road. Dead they thought.

Then one **of** the bankers had the bright idea **of** putting his green jacket **on** the kangaroo and taking some photos of it **with** his friends **in** their green jackets. So they lifted up the kangaroo and dressed it **in** the jacket. Then they stood **beside** the kangaroo while they took photos **of** each other.

But the kangaroo wasn't dead. It opened its eyes, jumped **into** the air, and hopped away **into** the distance, still wearing the jacket. Soon it was **out of** sight.

Unfortunately the key **of/to** the car was **in** the pocket **of** that green jacket. And all **of/Ø** their airline tickets and passports!

Using a dictionary

Vocabulary development

The extract in the Student's Book is from the *Cambridge Learner's Dictionary*. This is available online at **http://dictionary.cambridge.org**.

➡ This section will help students to develop their 'dictionary skills' and encourage them to use an up-to-date English–English dictionary, rather than a bilingual one. A dictionary like the *Cambridge Learner's Dictionary* is an incredibly useful learning tool, containing so many authentic examples and clear explanations.

1 👥 First ask everyone to highlight the occurrences of *at* in the story itself. Then they should do the task, referring to the dictionary extract.

Answers

She screamed at them – 3
at the top of her voice – 6
the sergeant at the desk – 1

2 👥 Careful reading of the dictionary extract is necessary!

Answers

He told us about his holiday	1
What about having a drink?	3a
What about you – did you have a good holiday?	3b
What was the film about?	1
He walked about the city taking photos.	2
I was about to phone you when you phoned me.	4
We got back about three weeks ago.	1

Extra activity – groups of three to five

1 Introduce this vocabulary memory game. Explain how it works and ask everyone to suggest what things Students C and D could say when it's their turn.

Student A: *Can I have an apple, please?*
   Student B: *Can I have an apple and a book, please?*
      Student C: *Can I have an apple and a book and a c . . . , please?*
         Student D: *Can I have an apple and a book and a c . . . and a d . . . , please?*

2 The groups begin the game, starting with the letter 'A' and see how far they get before they all drop out.

The rules are:

You must remember all the things and add an extra one. If you can't, the next person takes your turn and you drop out. (If there's time, play the game twice.)

3 At the end, discuss these questions:

• What letter did you reach before you all dropped out?

• Why is this game difficult?

• If you play it again how can you make it easier?

4 Change the groups for this more difficult version of the same game. (If there's time, play the game twice.)

Student A: *When you go shopping don't forget to buy one apple.*
Student B: *When you go shopping don't forget to buy one apple and two books.*
Student C: *When you go shopping don't forget to buy one apple, two books and three clocks.*

2B A better memory?

Can you remember?

Speaking and reading

1 👥 You'll need to set a time limit for the memory test. Two minutes should be enough, but be ready to extend this if most students haven't finished by then.

2 👥 At the end, ask for reports from some pairs. Which things do most students find hardest? Which do they find easiest?

3 Students read the 'blurbs', which are the publisher's description of each book, as they appear on the back cover. Then they decide which book they would prefer to read and why. Which aspect of their memory would they like to improve (spelling, ability to remember numbers, ability to learn a foreign language)? Which book would best serve their personal needs? They could also think about the style of the books. Are they old-fashioned or modern in design? Does the 'blurb' make the book sound interesting or dull?

At the end, ask the whole class for their verdicts – and reasons. What other information do they need to make an informed decision? (Number of pages, price, layout and illustrations, etc.)

4 This exercise picks some useful vocabulary from the texts and encourages students to guess the meanings of unfamiliar words.

➡ Highlighting vocabulary in context helps students to memorize new words and find them again easily. But just one encounter with a new word isn't enough to remember it. Further encounters and examples are required, together with a chance to experiment with using new words.

Answers

can't be trusted – suspect
dependable – reliable
obtained – gained
make stronger – strengthen
decide to learn from – commit yourself to

tested – proven
memory – recollection
being remembered – sinking in

Punctuation

Grammar practice

1 Although punctuation isn't 'grammar', we have included a summary of the main problem areas of English punctuation on page 120 of the Student's Book.

Some students may have problems with punctuation in their own language. If so, they should study page 120 very carefully!

2 First allow everyone time to guess the missing punctuation marks and pencil them in faintly. Then play the recording, pausing after each line for everyone to repeat the sentences. Warn them not to speak too fast and encourage them to imitate the intonation. At the end ask the class why the teacher asked 'Which tyre?' – to see if they understood the punch line.

Transcript and Answers 1 minute 20 seconds

Two students taking a chemistry class at the university were doing well in class **dash** they were sure they would get an 'A' grade in the final exam **full stop** Because they were so confident **comma** they decided to drive to another city the night before the exam to have a party with some friends **full stop**

Unfortunately **comma** they got back too late to take their exam **full stop** So they found their professor and said to him **comma**

quote* We **apostrophe** re very sorry we missed the exam **full stop** Our car had a flat tyre **full stop, unquote**

quote OK **comma** you can take the exam tomorrow **full stop, unquote**

quote Thanks **comma** Professor **exclamation mark, unquote**

The next day the professor placed them in separate rooms **comma** handed each a test booklet **comma** and told them to begin **full stop** Opening the booklets **comma** the students found just one question **colon**

quote Which tyre **question mark, unquote**

*Instead of 'quote' and 'unquote' we can say 'open inverted commas' and 'close inverted commas'. In American English a 'full stop' is called a 'period'.

3 ✎ This can be done in pairs, or alone, or as homework.

Model version (Some variations are possible.)

> **Remembering English vocabulary**
>
> There are many different ways of helping yourself to remember vocabulary. One method is to highlight each new word you see in this book. Writing words down in a notebook is also a good idea. If you do this, write a sentence using the new word, not just a translation. If you have a vocabulary notebook, arrange it so that you have a new page for each different topic. When using a dictionary, make sure you look at the examples, not just the definitions.

Ideas and reasons

Speaking

1 🔊 👥 There is a pause in the recording after each line for everyone to repeat the sentences. Warn them not to speak too fast and encourage them to imitate the intonation.

Transcript 1 minute 10 seconds

Man:	Bob writes new words in a notebook.
Woman:	That sounds like a good idea.
Man:	Why do you think so?
Woman:	Because it helps you to remember the spelling.
Man:	Oh yes, I see what you mean.
Woman:	Susan repeats new words over and over.
Man:	That doesn't sound like a good idea.
Woman:	Why not?
Man:	Because it's a bit boring.
Woman:	Well, I see what you mean. But it helps you to remember the pronunciation of the words.

2 👥👥 Two students look at **Activity 2** on page 131, two at **Activity 22** on page 137. Here there are more ideas for remembering vocabulary, people's names and phone numbers, and things they have to do.

Before they start their discussion the pairs should read through the ideas in their Activity and discuss them. Then they join the other pair and explain the ideas in their own words. Encourage everyone to use the phrases they practised in **1**.

At the end
Discuss with the whole class which seem to be the best ideas for memorizing vocabulary, and also grammar.

Different techniques work well with different people, so it's a good idea to experiment with a few different methods to see which suits you best.

Learning English

33

3 Money

3A Shops and shopping
3B Spend or save?

The aims of **3A** and **3B** are:

- to improve the students' ability to talk about shopping, clothes and money matters
- to revise the use of articles and quantifiers
- to practise the pronunciation of pure vowel sounds
- to practise giving opinions in speech and in writing

True happiness brings more richness than all the money in the world.
Too many people spend money they haven't earned, to buy things they don't want, to impress people they don't like. – Will Smith
Whoever said money can't buy happiness simply didn't know where to go shopping. – Bo Derek

3A Shops and shopping

Going shopping

Topic vocabulary

1 Make sure everyone knows how long they have for this discussion – at least three minutes.

At the end, ask for reports from different pairs.

2 The garments illustrated are:

belt   underwear (vest and pants)   zip   gloves   scarf   skirt   shirt   boots   jacket
tie   sweater (pullover)

3 Not illustrated:

buttons   coat   collar   cuff   dress   hat   heel   jeans   neck   pocket   sandals
shoes   sleeve   socks   sweatshirt   tights   trainers   trousers

Ask the class what other garments or parts of garments they would like to know the English words for. Can they identify everything they're wearing today in English?

4 Discuss any alternatives to these answers.

Answers

1 cash desk   note   change
2 earn/get paid   salary/pay   pocket-money/allowance
3 spent   window-shopping   credit card   cash   spent   market

Extra activity

Arrange the class into pairs for a clothes shopping role play. Half the class are shop assistants, the others are shoppers. In each shop there are two assistants and two shoppers. The shoppers should begin by writing a shopping list. The assistants can improvise what they do or don't have in stock. The shoppers go from shop to shop trying to find the clothes that are on their list.

Write some useful phrases on the board to start everyone off.

Useful phrases

I'm looking for a . . .
Do you have any . . . ?
I'd like to buy a . . .
Can I look at some . . . ?
How much does it cost?
I'm afraid we are out of stock.
We don't have any . . . but we do have these. They are very popular.
What size do you take?
Yes, we have these . . . they are 25 euros each.

Articles and quantifiers – 1

Typical mistakes

He's studying to be doctor.
He's studying the medicine.
She had a accident.
I went to the bed at midnight but I didn't go to the sleep.
The doctors are wonderful and so are the nurses (this is correct if we mean the ones in a particular hospital, but not if we mean doctors and nurses in general)
I'm learning the English.
English are quite reserved.
Have you ever visited the France?

1 As usual, studying the Grammar reference section before the lesson will save time.

2 👥 All the stories are about money!

Answers (Ø = no article)

1 **A** man in (**Ø**) Florida stopped **a** motorist and said he had **a** gun. He forced her to drive to **the** nearest cash machine. Then **the** man withdrew **some** money from **his** own bank account.

2 **A** man walked into **a** shop in (**Ø**) Illinois and asked for all **the** money in **the** cash drawer. But there was not very **much** money in **the** drawer, so he tied up **the** assistant and worked at **the** counter himself for three hours until **the** police arrived and caught him.

3 Police in (**Ø**) Los Angeles had **some** good luck with **a** robbery suspect who just couldn't control himself during **a** line-up. When **the/a** detective asked **each** man in **the** line-up to repeat **the** words, 'Give me all **the** money or I'll shoot,' he shouted, 'That's not what I said!'

4 In (**Ø**) California **a** man was arrested for trying to hold up **a** bank without **a** weapon. He used **his/a** thumb and **his/a/Ø** finger to simulate **a** gun, but unfortunately he forgot to keep **his** hand in **his** pocket.

3 👥 Ask everyone to discuss the questions after filling the gaps!

Answers

1   many   some   some
2   much   many
3   the   the   the

Vowels – 1

1　🔊 Play the recording. There is a pause for everyone to repeat the pairs of words. Make sure they say them differently. (1 minute)

2　🔊 Making sure everyone has their pencil poised, play the recording, pausing as necessary to allow slow writers to finish each line.

Transcript and Answers 1 minute 30 seconds
Presenter: Write down the words you hear.

walking	seat	beat	hat	match	Jan
working	sit	bit	hut	much	John
	set	bet	heart	march	Jean
	sat	bat			June

The answers are in **Activity 43**. Make sure everyone checks their spelling.

3　🔊 Play the recording – each sentence is spoken twice. Again, pause as necessary to allow slower writers to catch up.

Allow everyone time to read the sentences aloud to practise their pronunciation.

Transcript and Answers 2 minutes
Presenter:　Fill the gaps in the sentences with the words you hear.
1　iː ɪ　　Does **Jean** support the same **team** as **Tim** and **Jim**?
2　æ ʌ　　Isn't **Harry** a **lucky man**? Yes, but **Dan** is **happier**.
3　e æ　　**Fred** and **Harry** are **Jenny's best friends**.
4　ʊ uː　　Don't be **such** a **fool**! Don't **jump** into the **pool**! It isn't **full**!
5　ɔː ɜː　　Do you **walk** to **work**? Or do you prefer a **short** bus ride?
6　ɔː ɒ　　**George** loves **sport**. **John** likes in**door hobbies**.

3B Spend or save?

How much did you spend?

1　👥 We're going to hear interviews with the people in the picture.

Some things they might be saying to each other:
Those shorts are really nice!
What a lovely polo shirt!

Some things you might say to them:
Where did you buy those sunglasses?
That's a nice t-shirt!

2　🔊 Students will need to hear this more than once to get all the answers. Pause between each speaker to give everyone time to write their answers. At the end of the first listening, and each subsequent listening, ask everyone to compare their answers so far, in pairs.

Answers

	Julie		Bill		David		Teresa	
prices paid	polo shirt	£10	t-shirt	£5	jeans	£20	shorts	£18
	shorts	£20	CDs	£10	trainers	£20	sandals	£25
	shoes	£40	batteries	£2	sweatshirt	£15	sunglasses	£20
full prices	polo shirt	£20	t-shirt	£25	jeans	£40	shorts	£25
	shorts	£30	CDs	£30	trainers	£40	sandals	£25
	shoes	£80	batteries	£10	sweatshirt	£30	sunglasses	£80
total spent		£70		£17		£55		£63
total saved		£60		£48		£55		£67

Transcript 3 minutes 30 seconds

Presenter: Listen to Julie, Bill, David and Teresa talking about what they bought and how much they paid.

Interviewer: Hello Julie.

Julie: Oh, hello.

Interviewer: I like your polo shirt. Is it new?

Julie: Yes, I've just bought it – it was only **£10, reduced from £20.** And . . . I also bought these shorts – do you like them?

Interviewer: They're nice, yes. I like the colour. Did you buy anything else?

Julie: Yes, er…some shoes, but…um…mm…they were a bit more expensive. But they're really nice, look.

Interviewer: Oh yes, yes, yes, nice. So how much did you spend altogether?

Julie: Well now, let me see, **the shirt was £10, reduced from £20. And there were the shorts: they were £20, reduced from £30. And…and the shoes…um…well, they were £40. But they were the best value, a…and they were half price.**

Interviewer: Right, well, good, good. So…um…how about you, Bill? Is your t-shirt new?

Bill: Yeah, it was only £5 in a second-hand shop. Good as new, and good quality, look.

Interviewer: Oh, wow, yeah, well. What else did you buy?

Bill: Er…ohh…oh…um…two CDs, and…er…here they are, look. Ah…these are both second-hand too, I bought them in the market. And I also bought some batteries.

Interviewer: So how much did you spend and save?

Bill: Er…ooh…**the t-shirt was £5, but I've seen the same one in a shop for £25. Er… the CDs were £5 each, full price about, I don't know, £15 each, and the batteries were £2 for a pack of 20. The normal price is probably about £10.**

Interviewer: Well, I mean…looks like you saved a lot!

Bill: Yeah.

Interviewer: Um…well, how about you, David? Is your orange t-shirt new?

David: Haha, no, no, it's not! Er…**but these jeans are. They were £40 in the department store, but I got them for £20 in the market. Exactly the same jeans…um…for half price! Oh, and also in the market, I found some genuine Nike trainers and a really nice sweatshirt. Also both half price.**

Interviewer: Mmm, so what do you reckon you spent?

David: I reckon, well, **the jeans were 20 quid and so were the trainers. And the sweatshirt was £15.** So I saved…I saved quite a lot!

Interviewer: Yeah, I think you did! Um…well, so…w… you, Teresa?

Teresa: Well, I bought these blue and white check shorts. For my holiday! And also some new sunglasses and some new sandals. Here they are, look.

Interviewer: Ahh, very stylish, very nice. How much did you spend?

Teresa:	Oh…um…I can't remember now…um…oh, the price ticket's still on the shorts, hang on. Oh, **they were £18, reduced from £25. The sandals, they were £25 full price,** I'm afraid, but good value, they are. And the sunglasses, well, can you guess? Have a guess what they cost.
Interviewer:	Oh, I don't know: 50p – I mean £50?
Others:	Haha!
Inteviewer:	Only…only kidding! More?
Teresa:	Well, **these exact same sunglasses normally sell for £80. And I got them for £20.** Isn't that amazing?
Interviewer:	Mmm! Are you sure they're genuine?
Others:	Yeah, they could be fakes. They're not the real thing.
Teresa:	Haha! Well, you'd never know. And they look fine, I think.
Others:	Mmm. Haha!

3 At the end of the group discussion, ask various members of the class what they enjoy and hate about shopping. Are any of the students 'shopaholics'?

Giving your opinion

Speaking and writing

1 There is a pause after each line in the recording for everyone to repeat the sentences.

Transcript 1 minute

Man:	It seems to me that buying lottery tickets is a waste of money – what do you think?
Woman:	Mm…I think so too.
Woman:	I believe that the odds against winning are too high – do you agree?
Man:	No, I don't agree at all.
Woman:	Do you agree that gambling is terrible?
Man:	No, not really. I think that it can be fun sometimes.
Woman:	Don't you agree that some people waste too much money gambling?
Man:	Mm…sure, yes. I agree completely.

2 Using the phrases, each student in each group takes a turn. The others say if they agree or not.

3 The first paragraph is dull and doesn't have much to do with the title. The second is interesting, relevant to its title, and the style is more lively.

4 A brief discussion will help everyone to develop their ideas – and to decide what *not* to write. Fifty words is not very many!

5 When the written work is completed (probably as homework) put the students into small groups so that they can read and enjoy each other's work, and suggest improvements, before they hand it in to you.

4 Education

4A Schools and colleges
4B Happy days?

The aims of **4A** and **4B** are:

- to encourage students to talk about education with confidence
- to encourage students to write and talk about their own education and school-days
- to help students to talk about the past without making too many mistakes
- to practise the uses of the past simple and the present perfect
- to increase awareness of the use of collocations
- to encourage students to make notes before writing

What I hear, I forget. What I see, I remember. What I do, I understand.
Education is a progressive discovery of our own ignorance. – Will Durant
The object of education is to prepare the young to educate themselves throughout their lives. – Robert M.
  Hutchins
Education's purpose is to replace an empty mind with an open one.
My school-days were the happiest days of my life, which should give you some indication of the misery I've
  endured over the past twenty-five years. – Paul Merton

4A Schools and colleges

Teaching and learning

Speaking and vocabulary

1 👥 Allow plenty of time for this. If your students aren't very talkative, do this in groups of three. At the end, combine the pairs into groups to compare their ideas.

2 👥 Doing this with a partner encourages students to discuss the alternatives.

Answers

1 primary school   secondary school   leave   sixth form
2 strict   punished   naughty   detention
3 head   pupils/students   staff *(the last two in any order)*
4 marks/scores/grades   place   University   scholarship   graduated   honours

3 👥👥 We'll return to this theme in the first part of **4B**.

Past simple and present perfect

Grammar practice

Typical mistakes
I have been there yesterday.
When have you seen him?
Did you ever eaten oysters?

1 It's a fair bet that everyone 'knows' the rules for using these verb forms, but, just in case, there's a summary in the Grammar reference section on page 121. The list of irregular verbs (page 118) is also important here.

2 👥 This is just to remind everyone and help them to sort out any problems. Mistakes are underlined in the sentences below.

Answers

1 When <u>has she left</u> school? <u>Did she start</u> university already? (*Did she start school already?* is OK in American English.)
   When did she leave school? Has she started university already?

2 He <u>has started</u> school when <u>he has been</u> five.
   He started school when he was five.

3 I <u>enjoyed</u> learning English but I <u>didn't finish</u> learning yet.
   I enjoy/have enjoyed learning English but I haven't finished learning yet.

3 👥 **Suggested answers**

1 did you do   went   did
2 have you done   came/have come   am
3 Have   visited   went   had
4 was   played/learnt   stopped   hasn't played

4 👥+👥 Combine the pairs. Allow plenty of time for this as it's the most interesting part of this section!

Collocations – 1   Vocabulary development

1 👥 Some variations are possible.

Suggested answers

1 take   2 write   3 heavy   4 great   5 small

2 👥 Check that everyone understands the phrases before they do the exercise. At the end, ask for questions on the theme of collocations.

Answers

1 make   suggestion   do
2 make an appointment
3 good cook   do the cooking   do the washing-up
4 mistakes   make   did   work (*or* revision)
5 make   friends
6 good chance   do well
7 good time   good mood

4B Happy days?

My education

The written and spoken stories are models for what the students might themselves write and say about their own education.

1 Encourage everyone to guess the meanings of unfamiliar words from their context. These words might cause difficulty:

In David's story: scary   secure

In Sally's story: tease   naughty   cheeky   detention   gap year (a year between finishing secondary school and starting university – when many British students choose to work and/or go travelling)

Answers

	David	Sally
Didn't work hard all the time	✓	✓
Found it hard to make new friends	✓	
Was not encouraged by the teachers	✓	
Got bad test or exam results	✓	✓
Got in trouble		✓
Was teased		✓
Now works harder	✓	✓

2 🔊 Although the task is quite easy, students will need to hear the recording at least twice. There are special 'slowed-down' versions of these interviews on CD2, tracks 29 and 30.

We'll hear more from Andy and Rachel in **16B** and there's a photo of them there, which the students can look at before they hear these interviews.

At the end

Ask everyone for their reactions to the writers' and speakers' experiences. Which of them do/did they share in their own school-days?

Answers

	Andy	Rachel
Didn't like maths or science		✓
Enjoyed outdoor activities	✓	
Had to make friends at secondary school		✓
Has a twin brother	✓	
Liked English, geography and history		✓
Played tricks on people	✓	

Transcript 4 minutes

(Words that might cause difficulty are <u>underlined</u>. Answers are in **bold**.)

Presenter: Listen to Andy and Rachel talking about their school-days.

Andy: My name's Andrew Parsons; I'm a personal fitness instructor.

Interviewer: What sort of school did you go to? Or schools?

Andy: I went to…um…quite a lot of schools; my parents were <u>military</u>, my father was military, so we moved around a lot. I was also…um…an **identical twin**, or I have an identical twin, so…um…school was fun for me <u>regardless</u> and wherever I went I had my best mate stood next to me to get into trouble with and be good with, so . . .

Interviewer: So you were always at the same school and in the same <u>form</u>?

Andy: Al…always in the same school, but not necessarily always in the same form, you see, that changed. From sort of primary school we were always together, so…er…you know, it was double trouble, really. 'Terrible twins'!

Interviewer: And what about teachers? Any particular ones you remember?

Andy: I remember this one <u>guy</u>, there's a…well, two in particular. One…one guy was a guy called Mr…um…Thistlethwaite, he was a…he used to teach <u>vehicle</u> <u>engineering</u>. We used to…use to go in there and it was like a…you know…one hour a week. We used to go in there and <u>take</u> cars <u>apart</u>, which was quite interesting. Um…and I always really enjoyed it because it was just…um…it was just so much different to sitting in a…in a school room and writing essays. So…so that was fun. The other guy was a guy called Mr Morton. And…um…he used to teach outdoor education, so we used to go camping, ski-ing, windsurfing, we used to do all that sort of stuff and **I just…I just loved being outdoors**.

Interviewer: As you and your identical twin were at the same schools all the time, were there any particular memorable 'identical twin moments'?

Andy: Loads. Um…I think one of the things you get used to as a twin from day one, one of you is…ah…wears blue, one of you wears red and, you know, everyone . . . I always thought there was always this 'Top Ten Stupid Twin Questions' you'd get asked, like 'Do you wear the same clothes?'…um…'Do you eat the same food?' 'Do you breathe the same air?', all the kind of stuff that you could say 'No' or 'Yes' to. But…um…you get used to that but we used to do…I guess **we used to play tricks** a little bit. Um…if…if he would…had done something wrong he would blame me. They would ask me and I'd say 'No, it wasn't me, it was him.' So there was lots of that.

Rachel: My name's Rachel Babington and I work in public relations for a kids' TV channel.

Interviewer: And what sort of schools did you go to?

Rachel: Um…I had quite a <u>stable</u>…um…er…sort of school life really. Um…I stayed in the same town for my whole childhood, so I went to quite a small…um…primary school, and then when I moved to secondary school I went to a different one from most of the f…friends I was with because I went to a <u>Catholic</u> school…um…so **I kind of had a…a…a fresh start with totally new friends**.

Interviewer: And at primary school, did you enjoy it?

Rachel: Yeah, I did. I…it was quite a…quite a kind of safe little environment, it wasn't a big primary school and…and I remember, you know, having friends for quite a…a long time.

Inteviewer: Was there anything that you really didn't like?

Rachel: **Oh gosh, maths! Definitely. I was hopeless, absolutely hopeless at it.**

Interviewer: And what about secondary school?

Rachel: That was quite a big sort of <u>trauma</u> really because sort of leaving all your friends behind and doing a completely fresh school where everybody sort of knew each other, I found really scary. And after I'd settled in for about a year, I…um…after about a year I moved up to…a <u>stream</u>, so again I had to kind of start again making friends and it was all quite stressful.

Inteviewer: Um…what were your favourite subjects at secondary school?

Rachel: Oh, **I…I loved…um…English really**. English and I quite liked geography and history, um…but things like **science and maths**, where I really didn't shine, were my least favourite.

Interviewer: Have you ever been back to your secondary school?

Rachel: No, and I think I'd be really nervous to go back, I think it's a kind of scary thing to do, all those memories . . .

Making notes

1 👥 It's a matter of taste whose notes are preferable, but at the end ask everyone which they preferred and why.

Answers

David didn't mention:	Sally didn't mention:
played football	primary schoool – had fun and learnt a lot
was house captain	get job, then travel

2 ✏️ Set this for homework. And before the students hand it in, ask them to read each other's work and suggest improvements.

Agreeing and disagreeing

1 🔊 👥 There is a pause after each sentence for everyone to repeat.

Transcript 1 minute 10 seconds

Woman:	There should be no private schools.
Man:	I agree with that.
Woman:	I don't really agree.
Man:	I don't really know.
Woman:	Boarding schools are good for children.
Man:	That's absolutely right.
Woman:	Oh, I don't think so.
Man:	Mm…I can't make up my mind.
Man:	Children should start school when they are five.
Woman:	I quite agree.
Man:	Mm…I don't think that's right.
Woman:	I'm really not sure.

2 👥👥 Ask everyone to read through the list of opinions first, then they take it in turns to ask the others' opinions.

3 👥 then 👥+👥 After working out some ideas in pairs, the pairs combine for a discussion.

5 Relationships

5A Families
5B Love and marriage

The aims of **5A** and **5B** are:

- to encourage students to talk about family relationships and romantic relationships
- to revise the use of modal verbs
- to help students to use prefixes
- to practise using shorter and longer sentences in writing

All happy families resemble one another; every unhappy family is unhappy in its own way. – Leo Tolstoy in Anna Karenina

Why do grandparents and grandchildren get along so well? They have the same enemy – the mother. – Claudette Colbert

Parents are the last people on earth who ought to have children. – Samuel Butler

The first half of our life is ruined by our parents and the second half by our children. – Clarence Darrow

I've had bad luck with both my wives. The first one left me and the second one didn't. – Patrick Murray

A good marriage is like a casserole, only those responsible for it really know what goes in it.

Fear less, hope more; eat less, chew more; whine less, breathe more; talk less, say more; hate less, love more; and all good things are yours. – Swedish proverb

Life without love is like a tree without blossoms or fruit. – Kahlil Gibran

5A Families

Relatives

Speaking and vocabulary

1 👥 The photo shows a big family reunion: it could be somebody's birthday, or a silver (25th) or golden (50th) wedding anniversary.

2 👥 This is quite easy, but students unfamiliar with English first names may need some help deciding on the gender of the people.

Answers

1 daughter **2** mother-in-law **3** nephew **4** aunt **5** married husband
6 grandmother cousin **7** daughter-in-law **8** parents **9** twins
10 George and Ian

3 👥 The family trees in Activity 3 and Activity 23 have different people missing from them. The idea is for the students to find out the missing information from their partner by asking questions.

4 👥 If you feel this might be too sensitive for some students, suggest they draw the family tree of a popular TV soap opera – or an entirely imaginary one.

5 👥+👥 There may be other relationships, not covered in 2: step-brother, half-sister, great-grandmother, etc.

If students need help to get started, write these sentences on the board:

How many aunts have you got? Do you have lots of relations? Tell us about your relations.

Modal verbs – 1

Grammar practice

Typical mistakes

I don't can do it.
You must to do this.
You needn't to do that.
Do I must book in advance?

1 Before the lesson if possible!

2 👥 The incorrect ones are:

can   can't   may not   can

3 👥 Note that many variations are possible.

Suggested answers

2   can/could/may   should   shouldn't/mustn't
3   can't/may not/mustn't/shouldn't   can/may
4   must/have to/should
5   May/Can   have to

4 👥 Ask the pairs for their best ideas at the end.

Suggested answers

*On a plane, you can't use a mobile phone, but you can read a book and you must
    obey the Fasten Seat Belts sign.*
On a bus you can't talk to the driver but you can talk to your fellow-passengers.
*The driver of a car has to wear a seat belt and shouldn't use a mobile phone while
    driving.*
*Students in our school have to arrive on time for lessons. They don't have to wear a
    school uniform.*

Un–, in– and im–

Vocabulary development

1 👥 Your students will probably know most of these already, but if you think this may be tricky for them go through the first few with the whole class.

Answers

incapable	**in**expensive	**un**lucky	**un**sure
uncertain	**un**familiar	**un**necessary	**un**tidy
uncomfortable	**in**formal	**im**patient	**un**true
uncommon	**un**healthy	**un**pleasant	**un**usual
inconvenient	**un**helpful	**im**polite	**in**visible
indirect	**un**kind	**im**probable	
inefficient	**un**likely	**un**successful	

2 Highlighting **new** words will help everyone to remember them.

3 👥 There may be some imaginative variations – see **1** below!

Answers

1   unhelpful – *or* inefficient?   impatient?   unkind?   unsuccessful?   impolite?   incapable?
2   uncomfortable   **3**   unlikely   **4**   unhealthy   **5**   unnecessary
6   uncommon   **7**   impossible   **8**   informal

5B Love and marriage

Falling in love

Reading

1 👥 If possible, ask everyone to read this article before the lesson. (These genuine American children's responses to the questions come from a website article: 'Kids Say The Darndest Things'.)

2 **Answers**

1   Three – David, Bart and John   **2**   Two – Bart and Brad

3   One – Jeanne   **4**   Two – Lynette and Michelle

5   Mike (10), Tommy (5)

3 **Answers**

pre-school – kindergarten

lots of snow falling from a mountain – avalanche

good-looking (girl) – beautiful

good-looking (boy) – handsome

only on the surface – skin deep

spend a lot – pay good money

looking hard at someone – staring

pay the bill – pick up the check

4   **Finish the discussion by asking the groups for their favourite answers.**

Short sentences, long sentences

Writing

1   **The best titles are probably:**

Anna and Bob: *Absence makes the heart grow fonder*
John and Mary: *A love-hate relationship*

2   **Model version**

> Anna and Bob went to the same schools from the age of seven. They even sat next to each other in most of their classes. But when they left school, Anna went to college in the USA and Bob joined the Navy. They didn't see each other again until a mutual friend's wedding some years later. Soon after that they got married themselves.

3   **Model version**

> When John and Mary first met on a blind date, it was a disaster because they had nothing in common and they disliked each other. After four years they met again by chance. When they remembered their date, they laughed about it. So they had dinner and this time they got on well. But they still have big arguments. John asked Mary to marry him but she hasn't said 'Yes' yet.

How certain are you?

1 🔊 There is a pause after each line for everyone to practise their pronunciation.

Transcript 1 minute 20 seconds

Man:	Do you think John will ask Mary to marry him?
Woman:	Definitely.
	I'm sure that he will.
	When do you think he'll ask her?
Man:	Probably quite soon.
	I'm almost sure that she'll say 'Yes'.
	When do you think the wedding will be?
Woman:	Mm, probably in April.
	I'm almost sure that they'll have a spring wedding.
Man:	Why do you think that?
Woman:	Possibly because it takes a long time to plan a wedding.
Man:	I'm not sure if Mary will say 'Yes'.
Woman:	Maybe not.
	I don't know if she will either.
	Perhaps she won't.

2 👥 then 👥👥 If you think your students may not have enough ideas individually, this could begin in pairs.

1–5 Revision

The Revision exercises are fun if done in class in pairs. If time is short, some can be set as homework. The grammar, vocabulary development and pronunciation exercises could even be used as progress tests.

Topic vocabulary

Answers

1 Words from Unit 1

2 Words from Unit 2

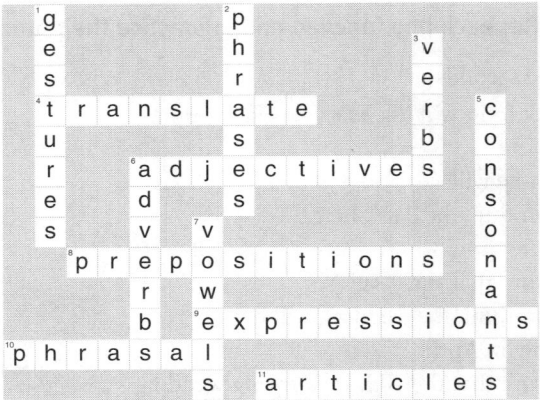

3 Words from Unit 3

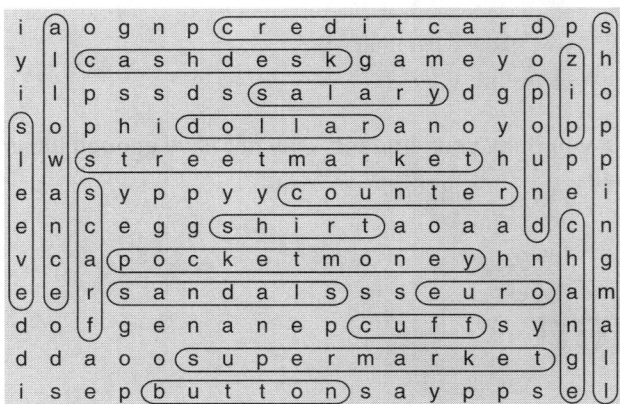

Grammar review

A Suggested answers

1 didn't do   went   haven't done
2 to   in   After   with   with   from   at   in
3 the   the   the   a   the   the   the   a   the   the   the
4 Have   met
   met   haven't met
5 have to/must   can't   have to/must   can't/mustn't   can/may   can't/mustn't

B Suggested answers

1 until it melted/turned into water
2 for the first
3 did the plane take
4 shouldn't make fun

Vocabulary development and pronunciation

Answers

1 one hundred and forty-four pounds   eight point eight   three and three-quarters
seventy-seven kilometres
2 marriage   relation/family   strict   shop/store   pay/salary/wage
3 bought · taught   feel · seal   gone · John   hill · fill   money · funny
one · won   said · head   through · blue
4 make   do   did   making
5 impossible   invisible   inconvenient   inexpensive   unnecessary   unclear
unlikely

6 Travel and holidays

6A The best holiday ever!
6B Travelling abroad

The aims of **6A** and **6B** are:

- to help students to talk about different kinds of holidays and tourist attractions
- to revise different ways of talking about the future
- to practise the pronunciation of diphthongs
- to introduce students to some different customs in other countries

A journey of a thousand miles begins with a single step. – Confucius
It is better to travel hopefully than to arrive. – Robert Louis Stevenson
The journey is the reward. – Taoist proverb
The man who goes alone can start today; but he who travels with another must wait till the other is ready, and it may be a long time before they get off. – Henry David Thoreau

6A The best holiday ever!

A great holiday

Speaking and vocabulary

1   👥 then 👥👥 Maybe point out that summer holidays can cover the whole period when you're not at school or college, not only the time you're away from home. Ask everyone to suggest some other equipment or clothing they'd need for the two holidays in the pictures.

Suggested answers

First picture:
backpack/rucksack   camera   fun   guide-book   phrase-book   sight-seeing
city tour   souvenirs   walking shoes

Second picture:
book   fun   sandals   seafood   sun-bed   sun cream   sunglasses   suntan
swimsuit   towel   watersports

2 👥 **Answers**

1 flight seat aisle took off/landed landed passport control
luggage/suitcase accommodation

2 breakfast half board full board self-catering all-inclusive

3 five-star single overlooking suite air conditioning balcony view

3 👥👥 At the end, ask the groups to share their most amusing thoughts.

The future

Grammar practice

Typical mistakes

I'll see you when you'll arrive.

The weather is being fine tomorrow.

If I'll pass my exam, I'll be happy.

If I'm going to pass my exam, I'm going to be happy.

1 If possible, ask students to look at the Grammar reference section on pages 122 and 123 before the lesson. The task reminds students that we can talk about the future using different verb forms – as the Grammar reference section explains. Here are the verbs highlighted:

Answers

One of these days, if I have enough money, I'm going to fly to New York. I'll probably stay with my uncle while I'm there.

– Oh, I'm flying there today on business. My plane takes off at noon.

Will you get to the airport on time?

– Oh, I'll take a taxi. It will only take half an hour.

What if the traffic is bad?

2 **Answers**

2	will be/is going to be	**3**	stops		**4**	'll close
5	does leave/is leaving	**6**	are going to tidy / will tidy			
7	starts/is starting	**8**	'm seeing / 'm going to see			

3 👥👥 Allow plenty of time for this, and ask for reports at the end.

Vowels – 2: diphthongs

Pronunciation

➡ Knowing the phonetic letters will help students when they look up new words in a dictionary.

1 🔊 There is a pause after each pair of words for everyone to repeat them. (1 minute)

2 🔊 Pause as necessary to allow extra time for everyone to write each word.

Transcript and Answers (also in **Activity 45**) 1 minute 30 seconds

		5	chair	**9**	share	**13**	mouth
2	really	**6**	rarely	**10**	Mary	**14**	now
3	like	**7**	lake	**11**	fear	**15**	fair *or* fare
4	hate	**8**	height	**12**	tall	**16**	hole *or* whole

3 🔊 Before you play the recording, ask everyone to read the sentences and try to guess some of the answers. In the recording each sentence is spoken TWICE.

Afterwards, the students should practise reading the sentences to each other, in pairs.

Transcript and Answers 2 minutes 20 seconds

1 eɪ   We all had to **wait** for **ages** for Jane and that made us **late** for the play. I **hate** being late.
2 ɪə   It's December: we're **nearly** at the end of the **year**.
3 əʊ   No-one **knows** what's going to happen **tomorrow** – until Tony **phones**!
4 aɪ   I tried to **buy** a ticket for a daytime **flight**, but the price was too **high**, so I decided to fly at **night**.
5 aʊ   'How do I get to the **town** centre?'
        'Go **round** the next **roundabout** and then **down** the hill.'
6 ɔɪ   Don't **spoil** the boys' **enjoyment** while they're playing with their **toys**.
7 eə   'Where's Claire? Is she **there**?'
        'She's **upstairs** washing her **hair**.'

At the end
Ask the class to suggest some more words that rhyme with the words in this section, and other words containing the same diphthong sounds.

6B Travelling abroad

Dos and don'ts

Reading and writing

1 In elementary schools and high schools in the USA, students have to say an oath of allegiance to the flag at the start of the day. That is what's happening in the photo.

2 To start off, ask everyone what they already know about the USA. How are customs there different from your students' country or countries?

3 **Answers**
1 false   2 false   3 true   4 true   5 false   6 true

4 **Answers**
¶1 stand in line   obey   punctual
¶2 hug
¶3 a positive outlook
¶5 uniform   civilian
¶6 critical   provoke
¶7 litter   tip

5 Ask some pairs to report their findings to the whole class.

6 For homework. (No model for this because the content will be different from country to country.) Students should read each other's work before handing it in to you.

Tourist attractions

Speaking

1 Expand the pairs into groups so that they can compare their ideas.

2 **Activity 4** gives information about St Paul's Cathedral, Tate Modern and the Millennium Bridge (right-hand photo), which joins the two. **Activity 24** gives information about the Tower of London and Tower Bridge (left-hand photo). Discourage everyone from reading aloud by giving them time to read and digest the information before they start sharing information.

You may prefer to have pairs looking at **Activities 4** and **24**, then joining another pair (to make four) as they share the information.

At the end
If there's time, try this role play:

Student A is a tourist guide to the place where the students live or are studying.
Student B is a visitor.
Role play a tour of the city or town.
Half-way through, change roles.

More about home towns in the next unit . . .

7 Where I live

7A Home, sweet home
7B My home town

The aims of **7A** and **7B** are:

- to encourage students to talk with confidence about where they live: their room, their home and their home town
- to revise *Wh–* questions
- to practise rising and falling intonation
- to practise using rhetorical questions in writing
- to practise asking and answering questions in conversation

A house is a machine for living in. – Le Corbusier
Always design a thing by considering it in its next larger context – a chair in a room, a room in a house, a house in an environment, an environment in a city plan. – Eliel Saarinen (architect)
The road to a friend's house is never long. – Danish proverb

7A Home, sweet home

Where do you live?

Speaking and vocabulary

1 👥 Encourage students to give reasons, not only opinions. Remind them how long they have for this discussion (about three minutes).

2 👥 The pictures show:

a	sofa	b	carpet	c	cupboard	d	blind
e	painting	f	reading lamp	g	sink	h	bookcase
i	desk	j	wardrobe	k	armchair		

3 👥 then 👥+👥 Pairs become groups for this. At the end, ask everyone how their homes
4 are similar and different.

Wh– questions

Typical mistakes

When you saw her last?

Why you don't like that film?

Who you saw?

Who did see you?

What means this word?

How you say this in English?

1 Deal with any questions arising from the Grammar reference section first.

2 **Answers**

2 Why did he fall asleep in the bath?   3 Why did they eat all the cakes?

4 Who broke the window?   5 Which town did they move to?

6 How many rooms does their house have? / How many rooms are there in their house?

3 **Answers**

2 is the oldest in the / is the oldest member of the / is the oldest person in the

3 does she / does your grandmother

4 long does it take (you) to get

5 often do you go to

6 will you visit her / will you go there

4 **Answers**

2 when the train arrives   3 (you) how old you are   4 where the toilet is

5 how long the film lasts   6 how I can get to town from here

Intonation – 1

1 🔊 There is a pause after each line for repetition.

Transcript with intonation marked 1 minute 20 seconds

Presenter: Practise saying these sentences.

Woman: Statements usually fall at the end of a sentence. ↘

Man: You mean like this? ↗

Woman: No, like this. ↘ But if a sentence is not finished, ↗ like this, ↗ the voice rises a little before falling at the end. ↘

Man: Do *Yes/No* questions usually rise? ↗

Woman: Yes, they do. ↘

Man: And statements that are questions? ↗

Woman: Yes, they rise too. ↘

Man: How about *Wh–* questions? ↘

Woman: They usually fall at the end. ↘

Man: Is that all I need to know? ↗

Woman: Yes, for the time being. ↗ But you may need to practise. ↘

2 🔊 There is a short pause after each speaker.

3 👥 Discuss with the class whether they are going to role play the same conversation or improvise a different one. An improvised one will need a few moments' preparation and rehearsal.

Presenter: Decide if the end of each line rises or falls in this conversation.

Man:	Where do you live?	↘
Woman:	We used to live in an apartment,	↗
	but now we live in a house.	↘
Man:	What kind of house do you live in?	↘
Woman:	It has three bedrooms.	↘
Man:	Do you have your own bedroom?	↗
Woman:	No, I share it with my sister.	↘
Man:	Your younger sister?	↗
Woman:	No, my twin sister.	↘
Man:	You have a twin sister?	↗
Woman:	Yes, didn't you know?	↗
Man:	No, I had no idea!	↘

7B My home town

Where are you from?

Listening

1 ◀» The photos, clockwise from top left, show Brighton, San Diego and Melbourne. Pause between each speaker so that everyone has time to make notes and compare their answers so far. (The Interviewer is Scottish, by the way.) There's a 'slowed-down' version of these interviews on CD2, track 31.

2 ▲▲ then ▲▲+▲▲ First play the recording again to show everyone how to structure
3 their discussion.

Answers

(There is more information here than the students are asked to write – they only have to put two nice things and one not so nice thing.)

Brighton	San Diego	Melborne
Nice:	*Nice:*	*Nice:*
close to London	lots to do	old buildings
seaside	lively	lovely parks
lanes and shops	beautiful beaches	old-fashioned trams
Not so nice:	*Not so nice:*	*Not so nice:*
busy with tourists in summer	traffic	winter can be wet and foggy
	scorpions, rattlesnakes	
Population:	*Population:*	*Population:*
150,000	1.2 million	3.2 million
Weather in summer:	*Weather in summer:*	*Weather in summer:*
hot	very hot	warm but not too hot

Transcript 2 minutes 40 seconds

Presenter: Listen to Mary, Tom and Brenda talking about their home towns.

Interviewer: Hello Mary, where are you from?

Mary: Um…I'm from Brighton in West Sussex.

Interviewer: What things in particular do you like about Brighton?

Mary: Um…I like the fact that it's close to London, that it's by the seaside, it's got lots of lovely lanes and good shops.

Interviewer:	Lovely.
Mary:	Um…but the things that I don't like about it is that it gets very busy in the summer with all the tourists. Um…and it's quite a small place, the population's only about 150,000.
Interviewer:	I see. What's the weather like in Brighton?
Mary:	Most of the time it's pretty good . In the summer it can be very hot, but it's very wet and rainy in the autumn and the sea crashes up the beach and it's beautiful.
Interviewer:	Thank you. Tom, where are you from?
Tom:	I'm from San Diego in southern California…er…which is a pre…kind of moderately medium-size city for America, it's about 1.2 millions, it's not too big, it's not too small. But what it means is that because it's that size there's an awful lot to do, it's really lively, it's got a big Spanish [-speaking] population so there's always…always lots of interesting things around. Um…and it's got beautiful beaches, you know, you can hang out on the beach and have a really great time.
Interviewer:	Is there anything that's not so good about San Diego?
Tom:	Well, there's not a very good transit system so, you know, you always have to do everything in your car. And that means the traffic can get really bad.
Interviewer:	Um…what's the weather like in San Diego?
Tom:	Oh, it's fantastic. I mean, it's hot pretty much all the time, especially in the summer it's very very hot, almost too hot. You can't really do anything without an air-conditioner and…um…you know, most of the time you just want to hang out in the pool.
Interviewer:	Sounds great!
Tom:	Haha! Yeah, it's not too bad, no. The down side though of that of course is, you know, if you're not careful you can find a scorpion or a rattlesnake in your back yard.
Interviewer:	Oh dear! Haha! Thank you very much. Brenda, where are you from?
Brenda:	I'm from Melbourne in Australia. It's actually…er…Australia's second biggest city…um…about 3.2 million people live there. I really love the life-style in Melbourne, there's a really nice feel to it with beautiful old buildings and lots of lovely parks, and these great old-fashioned trams that go all over the city. Um…probably the worst thing about it is the winter, it can be quite wet and foggy, and has a bit of a reputation for four seasons in a day.
Interviewer:	I see. What's the weather like in the summer time?
Brenda:	Oh, the summer's great. It's really really warm but it never gets that hot because it's on the coast. But…er…December and January are probably the warmest months, actually.
Interviewer:	Sounds lovely. Well, thank you all.

Why use questions?

Writing

1 Rhetorical questions make a text easier to read because they help the reader to see how a piece of writing is organized and they engage the reader's attention.

Answers
What are the advantages of this scheme?
Why is this a good idea?
What are they?

2 ✎ Discuss this with the class. Maybe point out that questions should be used sparingly. Over-use (of any rhetorical device) can look silly and is less effective than occasional use.

Discuss what kind of information the students might give in their e-mail.

Model e-mail

Hello Sam,

As this is my first e-mail to you, let me introduce myself and tell you something about where I come from.

Who am I?
My name's Alex Muster and I'm from Bournemouth. I'm an only child and my parents are both teachers. My Dad teaches maths and my Mum is a sports teacher.

What kind of place is Bournemouth?
Well, like Brighton, it's a seaside resort. It has a lovely sandy beach but it's so long that even in the summer you can get away from the crowds.

How do you get to Bournemouth?
When you come and visit me it's very easy to get here. There are plenty of fast trains from London and it takes under two hours. If you come by air, there's a coach directly from the airport to Bournemouth, so you don't have to travel into London.

What are the best things about Bournemouth?
It's quite lively, especially in the evening, and it's not too big so it's easy to get from one place to another. There's lots of lovely countryside around if you like that sort of thing!

I do hope you'll be able to come and visit me next summer.

All the best,

Alex

Asking and answering questions

Speaking

1 🔊 There is a pause after each line for students to repeat.

Transcript 1 minute

Presenter: Practise saying these phrases.
Man: Why do you like living in a city?
Woman: Well, I'm glad you asked me that!
Man: Why do people live in cities?
Woman: Ha! That's a good question!
Man: Well, let me think . . .
Woman: Let me see . . .
Man: Mm…I need to think about that for a moment.
Woman: What a difficult question!
Man: That's easy . . .

2 ✏️ 👤 then 👥  Maybe brainstorm a few 'difficult' questions first. For example:

Why is snow white?
Why is the sky blue?
Why do people fall in love?

3 ▦ Tell everyone how much time they have for this. Allow five minutes or so.

At the end

Ask the groups to report on their discussion. Ask them to justify their opinions – *'Why do you think that?'* – so that they use the hesitation phrases.

8 Entertainment

8A At the movies
8B That's show business!

The aims of **8A** and **8B** are:

- to encourage students to talk about films and other forms of entertainment
- to revise reported speech
- to practise the use of antonyms
- to practise writing a short review
- to practise ways of encouraging the other speaker in a conversation

> *Never judge a book by its movie. –* J. W. Eagan
> *We really need only five things on this earth: some food, some sun, some work, some fun and someone.*
> *It's kind of fun to do the impossible. –* Walt Disney
> *If you can dream it, you can do it. –* Walt Disney
> *I have a very bad feeling about this. – Star Wars* and countless other movies
> *Let's get out of here! – Star Wars* and countless other movies

8A At the movies

What kinds of films do you like?

Speaking and vocabulary

1 ▦ Students are free to discuss any of the *Harry Potter* or *Lord of the Rings* films – not only the ones illustrated!

2 ▦ Discuss the answers because many of these are a matter of opinion!

Suggested answers

positive: clever enjoyable exciting funny long (*if you like value for money*)
romantic? sad? sentimental silly (*if a comedy*) strange?
violent (*if you like violence*) worth seeing

negative: disappointing dull long romantic? sad? sentimental
silly (*if supposed to be taken seriously*) strange? violent (*if you dislike violence*)

3 ▐▐ This needs plenty of time.

4 ▐▐ + ▐▐ A happy ending is not necessarily unrealistic, of course!

Reported speech

Typical mistakes
He told to me that he was hungry.
He told that it was true.
She told me, that it was true.
She said me that it was true.
He told me that he will do it yesterday.

1 If possible, ask students to look at this before the lesson.

2 ▐▐ In case you're wondering, the origins of the movie quotes are given in the Answers. Students don't need to know this!

Answers
2 'I'm the king of the world!' – *Titanic*
3 'I am your father, Luke.' – *Star Wars: The Empire Strikes Back*
4 'I'll be back.' – *Terminator*
5 'Are you a good witch or a bad witch?'
   'Oh, I'm not a witch at all. I'm Dorothy, from Kansas.' – *The Wizard of Oz*
6 'Louis, I think this is the beginning of a beautiful friendship.' – *Casablanca*
7 'Remember that the Ring is trying to get back to its master. It wants to be found.' – *Lord of the Rings: the Fellowship of the Ring*

3 ▐▐ **Answers**
2 would make him an offer he couldn't refuse. – *The Godfather*
3 Major Strasser had been shot.
   to round up the usual suspects. – *Casablanca*
4 he was a Jedi like his father before him. – *Star Wars: Return of the Jedi*
5 they would always have Paris. – *Casablanca*
6 it had to be snakes. – *Raiders of the Lost Ark*
7 , after all, tomorrow was another day. – *Gone With the Wind*

Opposites

1 ▐▐ **Answers**
boring · interesting   bright · dark/dull   cloudy · sunny   complicated · simple
cool · warm   curved · straight   expensive · cheap   huge · tiny   long · short
narrow · wide   sad · happy   silly · sensible   slow · fast/quick   strange · normal
stupid · intelligent   weak · strong

2 ▐▐ **Answers**

1 short	2 heavy	3 strong
4 simple	5 beautiful/attractive/good-looking	6 expensive
7 a short time	8 cold/very hot/cool	

At the end

Ask everyone to note down some more adjectives and discuss what their opposites are. (Some have no opposite but we can usually say 'It isn't . . .' or use the prefixes *un–*, *in–* or *im–*.)

Think of some verbs too:

come · go   arrive · depart   raise · lower   lose · find etc.

8B That's show business!

Resonance fm

1 🔊 👥 Play the clip first. This is an extract from Reverso Mondo's show on Resonance fm.

Transcript (1 minute 40 seconds)

Presenter:	Listen to a clip from Reverso Mondo's radio show.
Announcer:	The time: the past perfect. The location: anywhere. Music runs backwards. You're listening into Xollob Parc. And here comes your host: R-R-Reverso Mondo!
[*backwards music*]	
Reverso Mondo:	Goodbye, everybody. Even with the savoury tang of [*name inaudible*] and his cheesey Latin sounds in our nostrils, we have to be going – cha-cha-cha . . . [*more backwards music*]

2 👥 This kind of task comes up in the FCE exam. It's quite confusing, but if students do it together they should be able to sort it out.

Answers

1 F   **2** A   **3** E   **4** D   **5** C   **6** B

3 👥 **Answers**

¶A   true   ¶B   false   ¶C   false   ¶D   true   ¶E   false   ¶F   true

4 👥👥 Once everyone gets going there's plenty to talk about here. If there's time, ask the groups to talk about the programmes they don't like too.

Your review

1 👥 These are model reviews for the students to follow. It's a matter of taste which one is preferable.

2 ✏️ Remind everyone that their review should be addressed to their fellow-students, who will read their completed work.

Encouraging the other speaker

1 🔊 Everyone needs encouragement! In a conversation, the other person's reaction is particularly important.

Answers

Are you with me? ✓	Do you see what I mean?	OK? ✓	
Am I being clear?	Right? ✓	You see? ✓	
I see.	Oh really? ✓	That's interesting.	OK ✓
Go on. ✓	Right. ✓	Sure. ✓	Cool.
Uh-huh.	Mm-hm.	Absolutely.	

Transcript (Answers are in **bold**. Other similar phrases, not listed in the Student's Book, but used here are <u>underlined</u>.) 2 minutes

Presenter: Tick the phrases from the list that the speakers use.

Anna: . . . I really like John Cusack, I think he's a wonderful actor.

Bob: **Oh really?**

Anna: Yes, if he's in a film I make sure I go and see it, **you know?**

Bob: **Sure**.

Anna: Did you see *Being John Malkovitch*?

Bob: Er…I don't think so.

Anna: He played the part of a puppeteer, called Craig, **right?**

Bob: A…a puppeteer?

Anna: Yes, a man who runs a puppet show, those little dolls on strings, <u>you know what I mean?</u>

Bob: Oh, **right**, yes, **OK**.

Anna: Well, he can't make any money with his puppet show, so he gets a job in an office in New York, **OK?**

Bob: <u>Yeah</u>.

Anna: But this office is only half a floor high, **right?**

Bob: Er…half a floor?

Anna: Yes, it's between two floors – this means that only very short people can walk upright. Everyone else has to bend over all the time, **OK?**

Bob: Yes, so what happens?

Anna: Well, he makes friends with a woman in the office called Maxine, and they discover a secret door in the office, <u>you see</u>.

Bob: <u>Yes</u>.

Anna: Um…and if you go through this door and down a long tunnel, you come out into the brain of John Malkovitch, <u>you know who I mean?</u>

Bob: The actor John Malkovitch, yes, but . . .

Anna: Hold on, let me explain: if you go down the tunnel, you enter the mind and life of John Malkovitch for 15 minutes, **OK?**

Bob: 15 minutes?

Anna: Yes, for 15 minutes you see, hear, and feel whatever John Malkovitch is doing, <u>all right</u>? And then you fall out onto a busy motorway. **Are you with me?**

Bob: I think so.

Anna: So he gets the idea of selling trips down this tunnel for $200 and it becomes a good business. Lots of people want to have the same experience. Oh, I forgot to tell you about his wife Lottie and her relationship with Maxine.

Bob: **OK, go on.**

Anna: Well, Lottie and Maxine . . .

2 🔊 **There is a pause after each line for students to practise.**

Transcript 1 minute

Woman: Are you with me?

Man: Am I being clear?

Woman: Do you see what I mean?

Man: Right?

Woman: OK?

Man: You see?

Woman:	I see.
Man:	Go on.
Woman:	Uh-huh.
Man:	Oh really?
Woman:	Right.
Man:	Mm-hm.
Woman:	That's interesting.
Man:	Sure.
Woman:	Absolutely.
Man:	OK.
Woman:	Cool.

3 Activity 5 gives the story of *Serendipity*, Activity 25 the story of *High Fidelity*. Make sure everyone reads the story through carefully before they tell each other about it. (Alternatively, they could prepare this for homework and tell each other the story in class in the next lesson.)

4 Some preparation may be needed. If so, maybe postpone this to the next lesson.

9 Communication

9A What do you mean?
9B Put it in writing

The aims of **9A** and **9B** are:

- to encourage students to talk about communication
- to help students to recognize how different tones of voice express different feelings
- to revise the use of gerunds and infinitives
- to give more practice in using verb + noun and noun + verb collocations
- to practise using emphasis and forceful adjectives and verbs in writing
- to practise hesitating and holding the floor in conversation

> *Never make fun of someone who speaks broken English. It means they know another language.*
>   – H. Jackson Brown, Jr.
> *The most important thing in communication is to hear what isn't being said.* – Peter Drucker
> *There is one universal gesture that has one universal message: a smile.* – Valerie Sokolosky
> *A laugh is a smile that bursts.* – Mary H. Waldrip
> *Start off each day with a smile and get it over with.* – W. C. Fields

9A What do you mean?

Faces and voices

1 👥 **Presumably the people in the photos are, from left to right:**

happy   surprised   sad   angry   terrified

Ask everyone to suggest other words they can use to describe the people.

For example: delighted/overjoyed   shocked   miserable/depressed   cross/annoyed
nervous/worried

Answers for 1, 2 and 3

emotion	face number	voice number	verb or noun
angry	4	1	glare (or frown or scream)
bored		4	yawn sigh
happy	1	5	smile laugh
terrified	5		scream
interested		3	smile
puzzled			frown
sad	3		cry · tears
surprised	2	2	gasp
disappointed			sigh cry · tears

2 🔊 **Discuss how each speaker could be interpreted differently. If you could see each speaker it would be very easy to interpret their feelings. Ask the class to guess what each speaker is talking about.**

Transcript 1 minute 30 seconds

Presenter: Decide what feeling each speaker is showing. One.

Woman: You don't understand. You're not listening to me. The whole point is that I wanted to record the programme and you said you'd set the timer. And now you're telling me that it's my fault?

Presenter: Two.

Man: Wow! I never realized it could do that. Y…you just press that button and the time sets itself automatically. That's fantastic, and all this time I was doing it manually.

Presenter: Three.

Man: Oh, really? Can I have a closer look?
Woman: Mm, sure.
Man: And what happens if you press this button? Oh, I see, yes. And is it necessary to . . . oh no, it's not, th…there's a menu on the screen.

Presenter: Four.

Man: OK. I'll just tell you how it works. You press this, all right? Then look at the menu on the screen and follow the instructions there. Any questions? No? OK, good. I'll leave you to it, then.

Presenter: Five.

Woman: Oh, I had such a good time! They gave me some lovely presents. But the best thing of all was seeing all my old friends again. It was so lovely to see them!

3 👥 Answers already given in chart.

4 👥👥 Finish the discussion by asking the groups to report back to the class.

–ing and *to . . . – 1*

Typical mistakes

To go on holiday is fun.
She avoided to do it.
I'm looking forward to go there.
She expected doing it.
I enjoy to play basketball.
I can't sneeze without to close my eyes.

1 Ask students to do this before the lesson if possible.

2 Answers

2	to understand	**3**	to answer/of answering	**4**	cooking washing up
5	to leave	**6**	Sending	**7**	to hear/to learn
8	coming				

3 👥 Many variations are possible.

Suggested answers

2 It's easier to talk to friends than to talk to strangers.
Talking to friends is easier than talking to strangers.

3 Listening to pop music is more fun than listening to classical music.
It's more fun to listen to pop music than to listen to classical music.

4 It's more fun to play basketball than to play golf.
Playing basketball is more fun than playing golf.

5 Flying to London takes longer than flying to New York.
It takes longer to fly to London than to fly to New York.

6 It takes (me) longer to walk to school than it does to walk to the city centre.
Walking to school takes (me) longer than walking to the city centre.

7 Sending an e-mail is quicker than sending a letter by post.
It's quicker to send an e-mail than to send a letter by post.

8 Going to the cinema is cheaper than going to the opera.
It's cheaper to go to the cinema than to go to the opera.

9 It's better to go by bike than to go by car.
Going by bike is better than going by car.

Collocations – 2

1 👥 Answers

answer a letter, an e-mail, the phone
dial a number
leave a message, a number
lift the receiver
make a phone call
open a letter, an envelope, an e-mail
send a letter, a message, an e-mail
write a letter, a message, an e-mail, an envelope

1 birthday card/letter/card 2 train/bus/bike/car
3 upset/disappointed/sympathetic 4 start/begin/end/finish
5 cost 6 take 7 last 8 question

9B Put it in writing

The man who invented e-mail
Reading and speaking

1 👥👥 Persuade everyone to read this before the lesson, if possible.

Answers

1 1971 2 Advanced Research Projects Agency 3 a unit price
4 30–40 seconds 5 He has forgotten! 6 none

2 👥👥 In some countries people celebrate their birthday, in others they celebrate their name day (the day of the saint whose name they share). In some they celebrate both: two parties and two chances to get presents!

Exciting writing!!
Writing

1 👥👥 Discourage students from highlighting too many words – they should only highlight the ones they want to remember.

Words normally used about food:
delicious, tasty – and possibly disgusting

2 👥👥 There are lots of possible variations here. Encourage the students to experiment and decide which words 'sound right' (i.e. seem to collocate) in each sentence.

At the end

Ask everyone to read their sentences aloud, sounding suitably enthusiastic or critical.

Can anyone think of more similar emphatic adjectives? *For example*:
atrocious delightful astonishing revolting ghastly

Suggested answers

1 brilliant/marvellous/lovely 2 a fantastic/wonderful/marvellous
3 love / am very keen on / am mad about 4 an awful / a terrible/dreadful
5 a lovely/great/wonderful 6 an amazing / a delicious / a marvellous
7 can't stand/loathe/hate 8 lovely

Writing task

Ask everyone to write two short paragraphs:

- one raving about something or some things they love or loved
- one about something or some things they hate or hated

Hesitating and holding the floor

1 ◀)) In the first conversation, the man keeps stopping and is interrupted and gets annoyed and frustrated when the woman keeps finishing his sentences.

In the second conversation, the woman uses suitable hesitation phrases and holds the floor. Then she yields to the man, who does the same. Their conversation goes well. Phrases used to hold the floor are in **bold** in the transcript.

Point out that hesitating is an important part of conversation, and not a weakness. Being able to hesitate effectively keeps you in the game while you're trying to think of the right word or organize your thoughts.

The alternative to hesitating (using *um, er, well, you know*, etc.) is silence. And silence seems like an invitation for the other person to speak.

Transcript 1 minute 40 seconds

Presenter: Listen to two conversations. Which goes better?

Man: You remember my old best friend…er…

Woman: Bobby, yes.

Man: Well, I met up with him the other…er…

Woman: Day?

Man: Yes, so I invited him to have a…

Woman: Coffee?

Man: Yes, coffee, and…and we started talking about…er…

Woman: Old times?

Man: Yes, when we were at…er…

Woman: School?

Man: Yes, we were in the same…

Woman: Class.

Man: No, not in the same class, the same team. We both played…

Woman: Basketball.

Man: *(sigh)* No, football. We were both in the school football team. Look, do you want me to tell you about this or are you going to…?

Woman: You know it's five years since we left school.

Man: Yes.

Woman: Well, you see, I'm thinking of arranging a sort of…er…reunion for…um…

Man: What? For everyone in the class?

Woman: **Yes, but just let me finish**. The thing is, I don't actually want to invite sort of everybody, you know, because, well, we weren't all friends, were we?

Man: No, that's true but if…

Woman: No, the point is…

Man: **Hold on**, I…**let me finish**.

Woman: Sorry, go on.

Man: Well, um…you can't decide to invite, well, some people and, you know, ignore others. It's, well, it would be…um…you know, very sort of rude.

Woman: Yes, I know, but…um…how…I mean, how could we sort of, you know, discourage the people we don't like to, you know, sort of not come?

Man: Hmm. Well…

Woman: I know! What if we…um…just…

2 ◀)) Students should try to copy the speakers' intonation.

Transcript 1 minute

Presenter: Practise saying these phrases.

Man:	…um…
Woman:	…er…
Man:	Well . . .
Woman:	. . . you see . . .
Man:	. . . you know . . .
Woman:	. . . and . . .
Man:	Just a moment . . .
Woman:	Hold on . . .
Man:	One more thing I want to say . . .
Woman:	Let me just finish . . .
Man:	There's one more thing . . .
Woman:	Oh, and another thing . . .

3 👥 Allow everyone a few minutes to prepare their story in **Activity 6** or **26** before they start telling it. They should try to use some of the phrases in **2** while telling their story.

4 ✎ To make a change, students could write the story they didn't tell but which they listened to.

10 Food and drink

10A Different kinds of food
10B Enjoy your meal!

The aims of **10A** and **10B** are:

- to help students to talk about the food they like, restaurants and cooking
- to revise different forms used to compare things
- to practise the pronunciation of consonants
- to practise explaining and then writing recipes

> *I will not eat oysters. I want my food dead. Not sick, not wounded, dead.* – Woody Allen
> *Our lives are not in the lap of the gods, but in the lap of our cooks.* – Lin Yutang
> *Never trust a thin chef.*
> *Some say the glass is half empty, some say the glass is half full, I say, are you going to drink that?* – Lisa Claymen
> *If you give a man a fish, he will have a single meal. If you teach him how to fish, he will eat all his life.* – Kwan-Tzu

10A Different kinds of food

Eating, drinking and cooking

Speaking and vocabulary

1 👥 This market stall, photographed in Naples in May, contains plenty of fruit and vegetables. Some are harder to identify than others, hence the question marks in the suggested answers! Encourage students to speculate and to use their dictionaries.

Suggested answers

herbs?		spring onions/fennel	garlic	yellow peppers	red peppers	lemons
radicchio	broccoli	aubergines		vine tomatoes		bananas
cherry tomatoes	carrots					pears
						aubergines
	bananas		lettuce (lollo rosso)	tomatoes	melons	strawberries
green beans + mushrooms? courgette flowers	basil? salad leaves? herbs?			courgettes	asparagus	peaches
					blackberries or blueberries	plums? or quinces? or apricots?
beef tomatoes			apples		cherries	
raspberries						

2 👥 There are lots of possibilities here. Take time to discuss them, and check spelling. Several possible answers are suggested, more than the students are asked to give.

Note that questions **4** to **6** require students to discuss their preferences once they've completed their lists.

Suggested answers

1 thyme　rosemary　parsley　coriander　cumin　allspice　nutmeg
2 salmon　sole　mussel　oyster　sea bass
3 lamb　beef　rabbit　duck
4 tea　beer　wine　lemonade　orange juice　hot chocolate
5 broccoli　pea　bean　potato　onion　courgette (US zucchini) aubergine (US egg-plant)
6 peach　nectarine　tomato　cherry　raspberry　strawberry　mango papaya　pear　melon

3 👥 The little pictures show:

a　knife, fork and spoon　　b　mug　　c　plate
d　cup and saucer　　e　sandwich　　f　saucepan
g　frying pan　　h　chopsticks　　i　bowl/dish

menu, oven and napkin are not shown

At the end
Ask everyone to suggest some more things they'd find or use in a kitchen.

Comparing

Grammar practice

Typical mistakes
Mine is gooder than yours.
Mine isn't as good than yours.
Mine is more better than yours.
It's the best of the world.
This is more difficult as that.
It's not enough sweet for me to drink.

1   Students have hopefully read the rules before the lesson.

2   👥 Discuss the possible variations.

Suggested answers

2   This is usually true.

3   That's not true. Sunflower oil is cheaper than olive oil / not as expensive as olive oil.

4   That's not true. Ice cream contains more sugar than fresh fruit.

5   That's not true. Cream contains more fat than milk.

6   That's not true. Margarine doesn't taste / the same as / as good as / as nice as butter. *Or:* Margarine tastes worse than butter.

7   That's not true. Carrots and oranges are the same colour.

8   That's true.

3   Again, discuss possible variations.

Suggested answers

2   taste as bitter as

3   not as sour as

4   more expensive than

5   more unhealthy than

6   (just) as healthy as / more healthy than

7   as bad for you as

8   is not / isn't as salty as

At the end

Ask everyone to write more sentences about food, using the same structures.

Consonants

Pronunciation

1   👥 This is not as easy as it looks. Most people are used to saying the alphabet from A to Z. Ask the students which letters are arranged differently on a keyboard in their language (if their language uses the Roman alphabet).

Deal with difficulties your students have with saying letters aloud: many students have difficulty distinguishing G from J and A from R, for example.

2   👥 Full, long names are more challenging than short ones.

3   🔊 👥 Before you play the recording, ask everyone to guess what the missing words might be. Check everyone's spelling afterwards. Each sentence is spoken twice on the recording.

Transcript and Answers 1 minute 30 seconds

Presenter: Check your answers.

1   Lamb is the kind of meat we get from **sheep**.

2   Do you have fresh orange **juice** for **breakfast**?

3   Give the **waitress** a good **tip** when you pay the bill.

4   Can I have a **thin** slice of bread, not a **thick** one?

5   When I eat **chocolate** it hurts my bad **tooth**.

6   **Yogurt** and **cheese** are both made from milk.

7   **Wine** is an alcoholic drink made from **grapes.**

8   When you follow a **recipe**, do you **measure** the ingredients?

4 👥 **Point out the pronunciation differences, as shown in the suggested answers, which are just a small selection of the many possible words.**

Suggested answers

[C][H] tʃ	chat catch chair which choose cheese
[S][H] ʃ	machine moustache champagne
	shake share push cushion fish sheep
[J] dʒ	joke juice judge jump just
[P][H] f	phone phrase pharmacy Philip photograph philosophy apostrophe
[T][H] θ	thirsty thick think through throw third bath earth north
ð	there this though brother northern with other neither
[G][H] f	rough cough laugh enough
(silent)	through eight thought brought
g	ghost ghastly

1OB Enjoy your meal!

Eating out

Listening

1 👥 **If their last meal was breakfast, maybe ask everyone to talk about a recent dinner or lunch.**

2 🔊 **Anna's talking about the third place, Bill about the second place, and Carole about the first place.**

3 🔊 **Pause between each speaker.**

Suggested answers

	Anna	Bill	Carole
Where?	England, in the country	South of France	Greece
When?	Spring	Summer	Autumn
Who with?	Three old friends from university	All the family (father's 60th birthday)	Girl friend
What did you eat?	Home-made ice cream	Barbecue	Fresh fish, grilled, + Mediterranean vegetables
Why was it memorable?	Four old friends meeting again after a long time	Everyone in the family was there	First day of holiday + best meal they had

4 👥 **This could be done in groups, rather than pairs.**

Transcript 2 minutes 50 seconds

Presenter: Listen to Anna, Bill and Carole talking about meals they remember well.

Interviewer: Is there a particular meal that you remember well, as being really good?

Anna: Um…yeah, w…we were in England at…um…at our friends' house in the country, and it was… it was . . . unfortunately it was a cold evening so we had to eat indoors. Um…this was in the springtime, and there were four of us, we're all old friends from university. And it was just a really lovely meal, I'll…I'll just never forget the home-made ice cream we had at the end – it was absolutely delicious.

Interviewer: Mhm. And…and what is it about the meal that…that makes you remember this so well?

Anna: Um…I think…I think it was…it was memorable because we were four old friends, you know, meeting after such a long time. It was brilliant.

Interviewer: Marvellous! Er…Bill, what about you? Is…is there a meal that you particularly remember?

Bill: Yeah, yes, that's quite easy for me, actually. We were in…um…France, the South of France, and…er…I just remember this fantastically beautiful summer's day, really hot weather. So we were able to eat outdoors in the garden, it was a stunning garden. This was in the summer, last summer. And…um…everyone was there, all the family, young and old. Um…and we were celebrating my father's sixtieth birthday, so we had a…a barbecue, and…um…it was cooked by my brothers, which is a rarity.

Interviewer: Uh-huh. And what is it about the meal that you remember so well?

Bill: Um…I think what makes it memorable basically is because…um…everyone in the family was there.

Interviewer: Mhm, lovely. And Carole, what about you? Have you had a particular meal that you really…really enjoyed?

Carole: Yes…um…yeah, it was in Greece…um…a seafood restaurant right by the sea and…er . . . oh, the weather was just really lovely and warm and so we chose to ate…eat outdoors. And…um…it was in the autumn but it was really lovely and warm. It was just the two of us: me and my girl friend. And…er…we had fresh fish, grilled, er…which was just delicious! And…um…and all sorts of Mediterranean vegetables as well.

Interviewer: Oh, that sounds delicious. A…and what is it about the occasion that you remember…makes you remember it so well?

Carole: Um…well, I think it was particularly memorable because it was the first day of our holiday, and we were just so excited about the next two weeks ahead of us, so…um…er…it, you know, and we had a wonderful holiday, but that was definitely the best meal we had.

Interviewer: Mm, smashing. Well, all three of you, thank you very much.

How to make . . .

Speaking, reading and writing

1 ░░ This needs a good five minutes. At the end, combine the pairs into groups for them to compare their favourites.

2 ░░ (It sounds much too creamy for me!)

Suggested answers

bake = cook in the oven
grate = reduce to shreds using a grater
sprinkle = gently drop a small amount
topping = surface

short-grain = not long-grain
shallow = not deep
dot = put small pieces

3 🔊 This conversation is a model for the students to follow when they explain their own recipes in **5** below.

Transcript (Phrases are in **bold**) 2 minutes

Presenter: Listen to Claire talking to Simon.

Simon: You remember that lovely rice pudding you made the other day?

Claire: Oh, yes. Yeah.

Simon: Can you…er…tell me how to make it?

Claire: Sure, yeah. It's…**it's quite easy to prepare**.

Simon: OK, great.

Claire: OK…yeah…need to…need to get the ingredients. **First of all** you will need…er…100 grams of short-grain rice . . .

Simon: Right.

Claire: About half a litre of milk. And about half a litre of cream as well. Er…you can use…um…less cream and more milk ac…if this is too creamy for you or you're being health-conscious. Or you could use only milk, actually.

Simon: Right.

Claire: And you'll need 50 grams of sugar, 25 grams of unsalted butter and…um…some freshly-grated nutmeg.

Simon: OK, so I've got the ingredients…um…so what do I do then?

Claire: Well, **then you** pre-heat the oven to 180 degrees and you butter a…a shallow dish for the pudding to go in.

Simon: Right.

Claire: And **first of all** you wash the rice and you place it in the dish. Um…and next you need to warm the milk and the cream together, and then pour them over the rice…er…covering it. And then you sprinkle…er…the…the sugar over the rice and you stir it all in.

Simon: Right.

Claire: **And finally** you need to dot…er… the butter over the top and…er… grate the fresh nutmeg as well over the whole of it. And you then bake for about 10 minutes.

Simon: Oh, right.

Claire: But after 10 minutes you need to reduce the oven temperature to 150 degrees and bake for a further one hour 30 minutes.

Simon: I see, right.

Claire: Yeah, and the pudding will now have a golden brown topping, with rich creamy rice pudding underneath. Lovely!

Simon: Mm. Sounds great.

Claire: Yeah, it's delicious! . . . **I hope you enjoy it!**

Simon: I'm sure I will.

4 👥 then 👥 + 👥 Some pairs may need help thinking of suitable dishes. A local speciality
5 is probably best, rather than an international dish.

6 ✏️ Students will need some time for this.

At the end
Make sure everyone has a chance to read other students' recipes.

6-10 Revision

The puzzles, and the exercises, may be more fun done in class in pairs. But if time is short they can all be set for homework.

Topic vocabulary

Answers

 Words from Units 7, 8 and 9

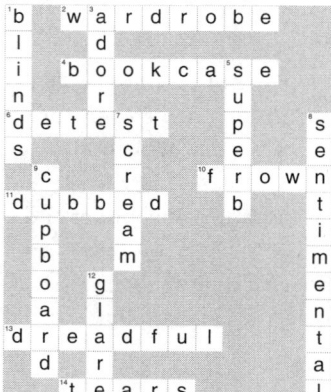

10 Words from Unit 10

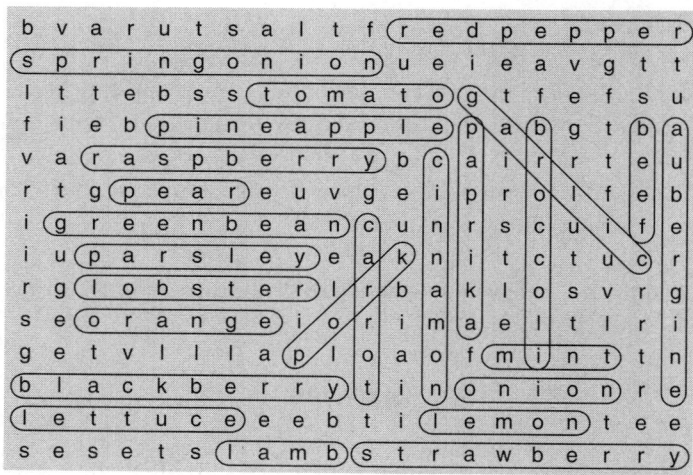

Grammar review

A Suggested answers

6 will go / 'll go / 'm going   go / 'm going   'll go to / will visit / 'll visit / 'm going to visit
go / 'm going   'll go / will go / 'm going   go / 'm going   will / 'll

7 will you travel / leave   will it cost / does it cost   will you / are you going to
will you go / are you going   did you go   did you   did you

8 (that) he was going / he'd been / he went   was   would have / could have found / got
(had) booked up   would go / went   would spend / spent

9 to travel   to   going / travelling   going / travelling   to meet   to get

10 as many   as   the same   harder / further / more difficult / more expensive   than
cheaper than   more   than

Suggested answers

6 does the movie begin?
7 did you leave the message
8 he had had a good
9 in going to the cinema
10 as much violence in *Harry Potter* as (there is) in

Vocabulary development and pronunciation

Answers

6 care · hair   crowd · loud   frowned · sound   fuel · jewel   my · fly
noise · boys   stay · may   quite · light   time · climb   wait · late

7 *What time do you usually get up?* ↘ — *On a weekday?* ↘
Yes ↘ , *on a typical weekday.* ↘ — *If it's fine* ↗ , *I get up early and go for a run.* ↘
And if it's raining? ↗ — *I stay in bed!* ↗

8 complicated · simple/easy   sensible · silly   wide · narrow   intelligent · stupid/dim
strong · weak   strange · normal

9 touch   send/write   take   make   dialled   answer   left   e-mail

10 age · page   lamb · jam   laugh · half   match · catch   push · bush
stamp · lamp   their · there   though · throw   worth · birth

11 Science and technology

11A Tools and gadgets
11B How and why?

The aims of **11A** and **11B** are:

- to encourage students to talk about their knowledge of science and technology and to help them with the essential vocabulary
- to revise the passive
- to practise the use of suffixes to form adverbs, verbs and adjectives
- to expose the students to scientific texts and encourage them to understand the main points
- to show the importance of a good opening sentence in writing
- to practise giving instructions

Most of the fundamental ideas of science are essentially simple, and may, as a rule, be expressed in a language comprehensible to everyone. – Albert Einstein

I am often amazed at how much more capability and enthusiasm for science there is among elementary school youngsters than among college students. – Carl Sagan

In science one tries to tell people, in such a way as to be understood by everyone, something that no one ever knew before. But in poetry, it's the exact opposite. – Franz Kafka

For a list of all the ways technology has failed to improve the quality of life, please press three. – Alice Kahn

It is only when they go wrong that machines remind you how powerful they are. – Clive James

If the only tool you have is a hammer, you tend to see every problem as a nail. – Abraham Maslow

11A Tools and gadgets

Great ideas!

Speaking and vocabulary

1 👥 then 👥+👥 The picture shows: a pair of pliers, a potato/vegetable peeler, a gadget for removing staples and a pencil sharpener.

2 Some more tools and gadgets the students might think of are: hammer, screwdriver, stapler, drill, saw, scissors, etc.

3 Students aren't expected to know these dates, the idea is for them to speculate and try to guess.

👥👥 Answers

dishwasher · 1886	by Josephine Cochrane in Shelbyville, USA: she wanted a machine to wash dishes faster than her servants could!
ballpoint pen · 1938	by Ladislo Biro in Hungary
colour TV · 1940	by Peter Goldmark in the USA
remote control · 1950	by Zenith in the USA to control their televisions
CD · 1965	by James Russell in Columbus, USA, but the first CDs were marketed by Philips in 1980
e-mail · 1971	by Ray Tomlinson in Cambridge, USA (see **9B**)
video recorder · 1975	by Sony in Japan: the first Betamax VCR cost $2295! The VHS format developed by Matsushita in 1976 soon became the world standard.
personal computer · 1976	The Apple I was released on April 1st by Steve Jobs and Steve Wozniak in the USA.

mobile phone · 1979	by Motorola in the USA: this was the first cellular network
Walkman · 1979	by Sony in Japan, but the cassettes they used were invented by Philips in 1963
World Wide Web · 1990	by Tim Berners-Smith in Geneva, Switzerland
DVD · 1995	by Philips, Sony, Matsushita and Toshiba

The passive

Grammar practice

Typical mistakes

The ballpoint pen was invented from Biro.
My wallet is been stolen.
I don' t know who by it was invented.

1 Students should do this before the lesson if possible.

2 👥 (It was Wilhelm Röntgen who discovered X-Rays, for which he was awarded the Nobel Prize for Science in 1901.)

Answers

2	were discovered by	3	were eaten by	4	was done by
5	was drunk by	6	will be played by		

3 👥 Many variations are possible.

Suggested answers

2	What is a corkscrew used for?	It's used to take out the cork from a wine bottle.
3	What are paper clips used for?	They're used to attach pieces of paper together.
4	What is a screwdriver used for?	It's used to drive a screw into wood, and to remove a screw.
5	What is a hammer used for?	It's used to drive a nail into a piece of wood.
6	What is a kettle used for?	It's used to boil water.
7	What are alarm clocks used for?	They're used to wake people up in the morning.
8	What is a dictionary used for?	It's used to look up the meanings of words.

⟹ Encourage students to think of some imaginative alternative uses. For example, a dictionary can be used to find out pronunciations, to stop papers from blowing away, to stand on to reach a high shelf, to support a short table leg, etc.

Suffixes – 1

Vocabulary development

1 👥 Deal with any questions arising from this presentation.

2 👥 Only the ones requiring spelling changes are given here:

Answers

funnily   easily   daily   loosen   natural   foggy   muddy   hungry   smoky
sunny

3 👥 **Answers**

1	sunny	enjoyable
2	particularly	useful
3	tighten	slightly

4	usually	sweeten
5	loudly	easily
6	emotional	suddenly

At the end
Ask everyone to think of some more words, using the suffixes from 2.

11B How and why?

Why is the sky blue?

1 There are no comprehension questions for these texts. The idea is for the students to face the challenge of trying to understand them without support from questions. The vocabulary task will help them to approach the texts with more confidence.

Students will need to have read and understood both texts in order to participate in the discussion in **2**.

2 Ask the groups to report back to the class.

A good start

Writing

1 None of the sentences has the same impact as the originals. This is mostly because of the over-simple structures used.

2 Collaborating will produce better results. If time is very short, this could be done first as homework and then discussed in pairs in the next lesson.

One, two, three

Speaking

1 This is a model for the kind of conversations the students will have in **3**, later. Play it several times because it only lasts a minute.

Answers

1	C	Find out Video Plus number in newspaper
2	J	Turn on TV
3	G	Press VCR button on TV remote
4	H	Press Video Plus button on video remote control
5	D	Look at on-screen display
6	B	Enter number of programme (not time)
7	A	Check it's correct
8	F	Press OK button
9	E	Press Exit button
10	I	Turn off TV

Transcript 1 minute

Presenter: Emma is telling Tony how to programme a video recorder. Listen.

Emma: Right, first you need find out the Video Plus number from the newspaper.

Tony: Oh, OK.

Emma: Yeah, and when you've got that, you turn on the TV.

Tony: Ha, sure.

Emma: Press then the VCR button on your TV remote.

Tony: OK, VCR, yeah.

Emma: And then you pick up your video remote control and you press Video Plus, the Video Plus button there, yeah?

Tony: Yeah. Yep.

Emma: And you'll see the information there, on the on-screen display.

Tony: OK.

Emma: Yeah? When you see that, you enter the number of the programme, using these keys . . .

Tony: Yeah…yeah . . .

Emma: See? Yeah. Not…not the time, just the number of the programme.

Tony: And I'll see that on screen?

Emma: That's right.

Tony: OK.

Emma: And you check it's correct, obviously.

Tony: Yeah. Yeah.

Emma: And if it is, you press the OK button here.

Tony: Uh-huh.

Emma: Mmhm, and then you press Exit button next to it on the right there.

Tony: I see, yeah.

Emma: OK? And if that's all done you turn off your TV.

Tony: Oh, great. OK.

2 🔊 The phrases in the Student's Book are recorded, but not in complete sentences (1 minute.) There's a pause after each phrase for the students to repeat.

3 👥 In **Activity 8** there are instructions on how to make yogurt, and in **Activity 29** on how to repair a scratched CD. Make sure students have enough time to study the instructions so that they know them well enough to explain most of the information from memory, not reading out loud.

At the end

Ask everyone which gadgets or machines they couldn't live without. For example, AA or AAA batteries – how much do we depend on them?

12 Around the world

12A Different countries
12B The other side of the world

The aims of **12A** and **12B** are:

- to encourage students to talk about different countries and world travel
- to revise the names of countries, nationalities and languages
- to revise conditional sentences
- to expose the students to authentic speech and help them to understand the main points
- to show the importance of a good final sentence in writing
- to practise contradicting people politely

No amount of travel on the wrong road will bring you to the right destination. – Ben Gaye
The world is a dangerous place to live, not because of the people who are evil, but because of the people who don't do anything about it. – Albert Einstein
How can anyone govern a nation that has 246 different kinds of cheese? – Charles de Gaulle

12A Different countries

Where in the world?

Speaking and vocabulary

 1 (All four photos show landscapes in Australia.)

Answers

Africa	Egypt, Morocco
Asia	China, Japan, Thailand
Australasia	Australia, New Zealand
Europe	Austria, England, Greece, Switzerland
North America	Canada, Mexico
South America	Brazil, Chile

 2 If there are particular local place names which are different in English and your students' language, write them on the board. (For example, for Italian students, Florence, Rome, Turin, Milan, Venice, Sardinia, Sicily, Tuscany, etc.)

Answers + **two more for each category**

countries	Holland Thailand	France Spain
states	California Texas	Michigan New York
cities	Venice Vienna	Milan Rome
counties	Cornwall Yorkshire	Dorset Kent
oceans	the Atlantic the Pacific	the Indian Ocean the Arctic Ocean
lakes	Lake Geneva Lake Michigan	Lake Ontario Lake Constance
seas	the Mediterranean the Red Sea	the Baltic the North Sea
rivers	the Nile the Rhine	the Danube the Rhone
mountains	Everest the Matterhorn	Mont Blanc Ben Nevis
mountain ranges	the Alps the Himalayas	the Andes the Rockies
islands	Crete Majorca	Ibiza Sicily

If . . . sentences – 1

Typical mistakes

If I would be rich I would be happy.
If I am rich I'll buy a yacht.
Life would be easier when I were rich.
If I'll see him I'll give him your message.
If I'd be rich I would be happy.

1 To save time ask students to read the Grammar section before the class.

2 👥 **Some suggested answers**

I'll go shopping if I have enough money.
If I don't have enough money I won't go shopping.

I'll go to the theatre if I can get tickets.
If I can't get tickets, I won't be able to go.

I'll probably stay at home if it's raining.
If it's not raining, I'll join my friends for a drink, etc.

3 👥 **Some suggested answers**

If you lived in Egypt, you'd have to speak Arabic.
If you lived in Brazil, you'd have to speak Portuguese.

Chile · Spanish   Taiwan · Chinese   Poland · Polish   Belgium · Flemish/Dutch or French
Switzerland · (Swiss) German, French or Italian (or Romantsch maybe)

and, more interestingly:

If you lived in Egypt, you'd be able to visit Cairo and see the pyramids and go in a boat along
    the Nile.
If you lived in Brazil, you'd be able to visit Rio and soak up the sun on Copacabana or
    Ipanema Beach.

Chile:	Santiago	take a trip to the Atacama Desert	go ski-ing in the Andes
	see the glaciers in the south		
Taiwan:	Taipei	go to a traditional tea house	eat fantastic Chinese food
Poland:	Warsaw	visit the old city of Krakow	see the city of Gdansk
Belgium:	Brussels	eat mussels	go to the old city of Bruges
Switzerland:	Zurich	see the Matterhorn	go up the Jungfraujoch railway

At the end

Ask some members of the class to share their most interesting ideas with the others.

4 👥 **Some suggested answers**

2 . . . I would buy an island in the Caribbean and a yacht.
3 . . . it would be hard to have a private life and avoid my fans.
4 . . . I would make it illegal for people to smoke in public places.
5 . . . I would find it much easier to make new friends.
6 . . . I wouldn't have to go to school and I'd be earning/I'd earn my own living.
7 . . . I would have to go to bed early and I wouldn't be so independent.
8 . . . I would have more free time.

At the end

Ask some members of the class to read out their best sentences.

Around the world

Nationalities and adjectives

1 👥 **Answers**

African   American   Asian   Australian   Austrian   Belgian   Brazilian
Canadian   Chilean   Egyptian   Indian   Mexican   Moroccan

2 👥 **Answers**

British   English   Polish   Spanish   Swedish   Turkish

3 👥 **Answers**

Wales   China   Greece   Holland (the Netherlands)   Japan
Switzerland   France   Germany   the Czech Republic   Portugal

4 👥 If your students are from a country like Portugal or Japan, ask them to add some other nearby countries.

12B The other side of the world

A different experience

1 👥 The photo was taken on one of Diverse Travel's trips into the Australian outback.

2 🔊 Warn everyone that this is going to be difficult! But if they can manage the task they'll have understood the main points. There are 'slowed-down' versions of these interviews on CD2, tracks 32 and 33.
(Words which might cause difficulty are <u>underlined</u> in the transcript. It may help students if you explain *some* of these beforehand. The answers are shown in **bold**.)

Answers

	Wayward Bus	Diverse Travel
Meet Australian Aboriginal people		✓
Groups of up to 21 people	✓	
See Australian animals in the wild		✓
Visit Kangaroo Island	✓	
'Hop on hop off' where you like	✓	
Trips last one day to one month		✓
Trips last 2 days to 10 days	✓	
Drive the Great Ocean Road (Adelaide–Melbourne)	✓	
Motto: 'Let the others rush'	✓	
Don't visit the usual tourist destinations	✓	✓

Transcript 4 minutes 30 seconds

Presenter: Listen to Ralph Jackson and Kristi O'Brien talking about their travel companies. First Ralph talks about Wayward Bus.

Ralph: My name's Ralph Jackson, I'm director–owner of a…a tour company in Australia called Wayward Bus Touring Company. Well, the theme is…er…small groups, <u>down-to-earth</u>, er…flexible, and we tend to mostly do <u>point-to-point</u> tours. You can **hop on in one place and…er…ride along for a few days, or even up to ten days, and…er…then finish the journey at another major…er…er…city.**

Interviewer: That sounds fantastic. How many buses have you got?

Ralph: We've got about 20.

Interviewer: What sort of buses are they?

Ralph: They're mini-coaches, taking **18 or 21 people** and…er…they've got cloth seats, er…er… tinted windows, curtains, air-conditioning, er…so…er…they're pretty comfortable and they're very tough…er…for…er…Australia's roads.

Interviewer: So do you go all over Australia?

Ralph: Er…Australia's a big country and there's lots of ways to travel around a big country and…er…our type of travel suits the area of Australia we're in. There's not a lot of public transport and it can be hard to find…er…the good places to visit. So we operate…er…between **Adelaide and Melbourne**, three and half days around…er…the famous coastline, the **Great Ocean Road**. And…er…we run eight and **ten day tours** between Adelaide and Alice Springs. We also do…um…er…short tours, **two days**, three days down to **Kangaroo Island** from Adelaide.

Interviewer: And what sort of age group are the people?

Ralph: Most of our travellers are in their twenties and thirties…er…but…er…there's no age restrictions, and…oh…er…kids are welcome, um…oldies are welcome, so we tend to get people who are looking for something that's…er…active, down-to-earth, er . . .

Interviewer: I was going to say, how do…how are your trips different from the normal kind of trips that people might take on…on a holiday?

Ralph: Our motto is '**Let the others rush**'. Er…so we take our time, we…we tend to…um…spend more time at places, er…drive less distance in a day than a lot of the…um…bigger coach tours. And…um…**we can go to…er…places that are more out of the way**.

Presenter: Now Kristi talks about Diverse Travel.

Kristi: My name is Kristi O'Brien and I'm the managing director of a company called Diverse Travel Australia. Diverse Travel Australia…um…specializes in connecting people to Aboriginal experiences found throughout Australia, um…sending people to wonderful nature-based locations throughout Australia.

Interviewer: How long do your trips last?

Kristi: Oh, they can last anywhere **from a day through to…er…a month**. We've never done anything beyond a month.

Interviewer: And what sort of people come on your trip?

Kristi: They're people that…er…are wanting to get to know the real Australia and meet its local characters and go into some of its **lesser-known destinations, away from the mainstream tourist trap**.

Interviewer: Why do you think tourists choose your kind of trip?

Kristi: There's a lot of people, even first-time travellers that want to really get to know what makes a country tick. Like meet the local people, **see the wildlife out in the wilds of Australia**, and…um…it's those sort of people that our company appeals to.

Interviewer: How do they react going into an Aboriginal culture?

Kristi: We try to educate them a little bit before they go in. Sometimes it's not good to look Aboriginal people in the eyes. They can be quite shy, reserved, so we have to sort of teach them [*the tourists*] a little bit about some of the cultures they'll be going into. The more you go into the outback areas, which is the desert areas, the…or, you know, the less contact a lot of the Aboriginal people have had with European or non-Aboriginal people. So yeah, it's interesting watching different cultures slowly sort of interact with the **Aboriginal people**.

Interviewer: And the experiences presumably are very positive.

Kristi: I think in our fast-paced life in Western society we forget I think what life is truly about.

Interviewer: And do you work with Aboriginal guides?

Kristi: Oh yes, throughout Australia.

Interviewer: Now what do…er…some of your visitors…or…what surprises them?

Kristi: I think…um…our wildlife surprises them. I think the open space, not seeing people for miles surprises them. I think lots of nothing surprises them and the incredible distances that has to…have to be travelled in Australia to get anywhere.

3 ⏸ After a few minutes, combine the pairs into groups – or continue the discussion as a whole class.

A good ending   Writing

1 ⏸ The sentences are less effective (and less dramatic) than the originals mainly because of the arrangement of ideas. The originals all seem to round off the text in a more satisfying way.

2 ✎ ⏸ This should be started together in pairs even if the actual rewriting is done as homework.

That's not right!   Speaking

1 ◀)) Maybe point out that it's not only a question of whether you know someone well that determines how directly you can contradict them – you also have to take into account how sensitive they are! Also, students should be very careful using sarcasm, even with people they know quite well, in case it's misinterpreted.

Answers

	to Betty	to Mrs Frost
I'm sorry, that's not right.		✓
I don't think that's right.		✓
Are you quite sure about that?		✓
I'm not sure that's right.		✓
I don't think so.	✓	✓
That's completely wrong!	✓	
No, you're wrong!	✓	
That's nonsense!	✓	
Don't be so silly!	✓	

Transcript 1 minute 20 seconds

Presenter: Tony is talking to Betty, a good friend, and to Mrs Frost, an older acquaintance.

Betty: . . . so Sydney is the capital of Australia.
Tony: That's completely wrong!

Mrs Frost: . . . because, well, Melbourne is the capital of Australia.
Tony: I'm sorry, that's not right.
Mrs Frost: Oh, in that case it must be Perth.
Tony: I'm not sure that's right.

Betty: . . . I'm sure that a mile is the same as a kilometre.
Tony: No, you're wrong!

Mrs Frost: . . . I thought that a kilometre was the same as a mile.
Tony: I don't think that's right.

Betty:	. . . I know that New Zealand is bigger than Australia.
Tony:	That's nonsense! Don't be so silly!
Mrs Frost:	. . . and then someone told me that Australia is smaller than New Zealand.
Tony:	Are you quite sure about that?
Mrs Frost:	. . . you see, I'm sure they speak French in Australia.
Tony:	(*politely*) I don't think so.
Betty:	. . . it's true that everyone speaks Greek in Australia.
Tony:	(*sarcastically*) I don't think so.

2 🔊 **The phrases on the right are recorded for pronunciation practice. (40 seconds.) There's a pause after each phrase for the students to repeat.**

3 👤 then 👥 **If students are not keen on geography, they can write ten untrue sentences about other subjects instead.**

At the end
Write some untrue statements of you own and invite the class to contradict you – politely!

13 Weather and climate

13A Lovely weather!
13B Terrible weather

The aims of **13A** and **13B** are:

- to encourage students to talk about weather and climate
- to revise reported questions
- to practise using suffixes to form nouns
- to practise writing about personal experiences
- to practise asking for clarification in conversation

> *Don't knock the weather. If it didn't change once in a while, nine out of ten people couldn't start a conversation.* – Kin Hubbard
> *A good laugh is sunshine in a house.* – William Makepeace Thackeray

13A Lovely weather!

What's the weather going to be like?

1 🔊 👥 **Suggested answers**

SATURDAY	weather	temp
morning	dry, cloudy	15°
lunchtime	brighter	20°
afternoon	rain	13°
evening	rain	10°
overnight	rain	8°

SUNDAY	weather	temp
morning	wet, cool	12°
lunchtime	clear, sunny	15°
afternoon	sunny	25°
evening	clear	20°
overnight	dry	15°

Transcript (Answers are in **bold**.) 1 minute 50 seconds.

Presenter: Listen to two weather forecasts. The first is for Saturday.

Anna (newsreader): . . . everything arrived perfectly in one piece and so the dog's owners were very pleased. And now Saturday's weather from Peter Storm. Peter.

Peter (weather forecaster): Thank you, Anna. Well, it's a story of rain and cool weather, I'm afraid.

Anna: Oh, no!

Peter: Yes, the rain will arrive later in the day, so the morning will be **dry but cloudy**, with a temperature of **15** degrees. Then at lunchtime it will become **brighter** and it could rise to **20** degrees. I'm afraid after lunch the **rain** will arrive and the temperature will drop to around **13** degrees. As the evening wears on the **rain** will persist and the temperature will fall to **10** degrees. Then overnight it will continue to **rain** and the temperature may go down as low as **8** degrees. Pretty cold for the time of year, I'm afraid. So…ah…that's all from me.

Presenter: The second weather forecast is for Sunday.

Bill (newsreader): . . . and the children all arrived safe and sound. And now the weather for Sunday from Tracy. Here's Tracy.

Tracy (weather forecaster): Yes, Bill, well, the morning will s…start **wet and cool**, temperature about **12 degrees**. But as the day goes on the rain will stop and the **sun** will come out. So by lunchtime it'll be **clear** and warmer, about **15** degrees. Then in the afternoon, the **sun** will shine brightly and it will become much warmer: as warm as **25** degrees by the end of the afternoon. Then a…a lovely evening, **clear** skies, temperature **20** degrees. Overnight staying **dry**, temperature around **15** degrees. Then the outlook for Monday and the rest of the week: staying dry and getting even warmer!

Bill: Oh, lovely!

Tracy: That's about it from me.

2 👥 **Possible variations will be discussed in 3.**

Suggested answers

Rain is when drops of water fall from the clouds; **drizzle** is fine rain in tiny drops.

A **hot day** is a day when the temperature is high; a **heatwave** is a whole series of very hot days.

A **shower** is when rain falls for a few minutes; a **downpour** is a very heavy shower.

A **breeze** is a light wind; a **gale** is a very strong wind.

Weather and climate

A **cloud** is a white or grey mass of tiny drops of water floating in the sky; **fog** is a cloud at ground level.

Frost is what you get when the temperature falls below freezing; **ice** is frozen water on a lake, for example.

3 👥+👥 The pairs join up to compare answers and talk about their own experiences and opinions.

Reported questions

Grammar practice

Typical mistakes

He asked me if it will rain.
She wanted to know when would it rain.
She asked to me when I would arrive.
She wants to know what is the answer.

1 Ask students to look at this before they come to class, if possible. This exercise requires students to form groups of three.

2 🔊👤 then 👥👥 The recording shows students what they have to do.

Transcript 40 seconds

Presenter:	Listen to the examples.
Alex (to Beth):	Er…What's the weather going to be like tomorrow? Ask Charlie for me.
Beth (to Charlie):	Alex wants to know what the weather is going to be like tomorrow.
Charlie (to Beth):	I think it's going to be hot.
Beth (to Alex):	Charlie says he thinks it's going to be hot.
Alex (to Beth):	OK. Now ask Charlie a question and he'll ask me.
Beth (to Charlie):	Right, Charlie. Find out what time Alex left home this morning.
Charlie (to Alex):	Alex, what time did you leave home this morning? . . .

3 👥 **Suggested answers**

2 if I would be free to come / go out with them / her and her friends.
3 if I had seen his pen anywhere.
4 where her bag was.
5 if/whether she/he wanted me to look for it.
6 how long the exercise would take.
7 me why I was sitting in the dark.

4 👥👥 Now that time has elapsed, the questions that were asked in **2** are now in the past, as the example shows! Students should work in groups of three.

Suffixes – 2: nouns

Vocabulary development

1 👥 Deal with any questions before doing **2**.

2 👥 **Answers**

(Only the words with changes in spelling are given here.)

–er	driver	manager
–or	narrator	
–ist	pianist	scientist

–er	timer				
–ness	friendliness	loneliness			
–ity	sincerity	severity			
–ence	difference	confidence	innocence	patience	violence
–ance	insurance				
–ion	investigation	operation			
–ation	explanation	examination	organization		
–ing	typing				

3 👥 **Suggested answers**

1 artist/painter Movement enjoyment paintings
2 operations patience training
3 investigation disappearance seriousness reaction explanation
4 driver carelessness insurance payment

At the end
Ask the class if they can think of more words using the same suffixes.

13B Terrible weather

Weather chaos

Reading

1 👥 The infinitive in a headline shows a future event or prediction. The simple present shows a past event (*El Niño brings chaos*).

2 **Suggested answers**

1 More than 9 (China, Honduras, India, Bangladesh, the USA, Indonesia, Brazil, Florida, California and Mexico are mentioned by name. But large regions are also mentioned: Latin America, southern Africa, the Pacific region and Europe, so there were far more than just 9 affected.)
2 Thousands
3 An increase in cloudiness and rainfall over the equatorial central Pacific
4 The tropical Pacific
5 Every two to ten years

3 **Answers**

¶1 periodic trigger
¶2 droughts floods
¶3 devastated
¶4 provoke devastating
¶7 impacts
¶8 occurred

4 👥 Ask the pairs to report back to the class.

Personal experiences

Writing

1 👥 This discussion will provide material for the writing practice in 2.

2 ✎ If this is done in class, the students can share their best sentences with each other.

3 ✎ Hopefully some students will have more dramatic stories to tell than the model version.

Model version

Dear Max,

I've just got back from holiday. And what a time we had! The day we arrived there was a downpour which flooded the campsite and we had to sleep in the car. It took all the next day to clear up the mess that the water had caused and the ground was still too wet for us to put up our tent. Luckily, there were some people in a camper van who wanted to spend the night in a hotel, so they let us sleep in their van.

After that first day the sun never stopped shining! The campsite dried out completely and the temperature rose and rose. At the end of the week it was in the mid-thirties! We had to sit in the shade in the afternoon and we certainly needed the factor 30 suncream the rest of the day. It was even so hot at night that we found it hard to sleep. Don't think I'm complaining, because we had a great time.

How was your holiday? Write and tell me about it.

Love,

Amy

P.S. Did you get the postcard I sent you?

How do you mean?

Speaking

1 🔊 The conversation shows the students how the phrases can be used.

Transcript and Answers 1 minute

Presenter: Listen to David and Karen. Which of the phrases do they use?

David: . . . and every snowflake is different.
Karen: **In what way?**
David: **I mean** the crystal structure of every single flake of snow is unique.
Karen: Oh, **I don't quite understand**, sorry.
David: W…**what I mean is**: you know that snow is formed of crystals, don't you?
Karen: Crystals? Er…no, I thought they were sort of solid grains.
David: No, if you see one magnified, you can see it's a very beautiful arrangement of tiny pieces of ice.
Karen: Er…**I don't see what you mean**. Ice is solid, surely?
David: Yes, but snow is lots of tiny pieces of ice all joined together.
Karen: I see, but if snow is ice . . .

2 🔊 The phrases are recorded for pronunciation practice (40 seconds).

3 👥 The prompts in Activity 14 and Activity 40 provide more ideas for a discussion about different kinds of weather, and personal experiences and opinions.

Weather and climate

14 Nature

14A Living creatures
14B The environment

The aims of **14A** and **14B** are:

- to encourage students to talk about nature and the environment
- to revise the past simple and past continuous
- to practise the use of abbreviations and symbols
- to practise comparing things in writing
- to practise using follow-up questions in conversation

It's a wonderful world – Louis Armstrong

It is not the strongest of the species that survives, nor the most intelligent that survives. It is the one that is the most adaptable to change. – Charles Darwin

You can say any fool thing to a dog, and the dog will give you this look that says, 'My God, you're right! I never would've thought of that!' – Dave Barry

14A Living creatures

It's a wonderful world!

Speaking and vocabulary

1 👥 Encourage students to give reasons for their answers to the first two questions.

2 👥 **Some suggested answers**

wild animals:	deer	tiger	lion	hare	bear	kangaroo
farm animals:	goat	pig	chicken	horse	donkey	
birds:	sparrow	pigeon	vulture	eagle	seagull	
insects:	wasp	beetle	cockroach	fly	mosquito	butterfly
fish:	trout	sea bass	tuna	sole	sardine	anchovy
reptiles:	lizard	alligator	turtle	iguana	tortoise	
trees:	maple	pine	apple	olive	cypress	beech
fruit:	blackberry	strawberry	raspberry	peach	pear	plum
flowers:	daisy	dandelion	camellia	daffodil	orchid	

3 👥 then 👥+👥 This should lead to some lively discussion about who is the 'greenest'.
4

Past simple and past continuous

Grammar practice

Typical mistakes

He drank tea when the lights went out.
We were hearing a crash while he did the washing-up.
She was dropping a glass on the floor.
I sat alone reading a book when the lights were going out.

1 Before the lesson, if possible.

2 Suggested answers

2 I was watching TV in the living room.
I let it ring because I didn't want to miss the programme.

3 I was sitting all alone reading a book.
I wondered who was at the door, so I shouted out, 'Who is it?'

4 I was eating my dinner.
I went on eating in the dark.

3 👥 Make sure everyone looks at the examples before they start, and answer any questions students have about them.

Abbreviations and symbols, etc.

1 👥 **Suggested answers**

Mister   /ˈmɪsɪz/   Doctor   Professor
Avenue   Drive   Gardens   Road   Square   Street
am /eɪem/   pm /piːem/   hours   maximum   minimum   approximately
metres   kilograms
compact disc   television   digital versatile disc   video cassette recorder/video recorder
personal computer   World Wide Web
United States of America   United Kingdom   Great Britain   European Union
United Nations   /neɪtəʊ/ North Atlantic Treaty Organization
World Wide Fund for Nature
and   dollar   pound   per cent   dash   slash   copyright   registered trademark
zero   at   degrees Celsius

2 👥 **Answers**
Tue   Wed   Thu   Fri   Sat
Mar   Apr   May   Jun   Jul   Aug   Sep   Oct   Nov   Dec

3 👥 These could be government organizations, companies or addresses which people from another country might not understand – hence the task of explaining their meanings in English.

14B The environment

The Eden Project

1 👥 Deal with any questions arising from reading the text. Has anyone heard of the Eden Project before?

2 🔊 Play the first 30 seconds or so of the interview, then rewind to the beginning, so that the students can start to get used to Sue's voice and her speed of delivery. There's a 'slowed-down' version of this interview on CD2, track 34.
(Words which might cause difficulty are <u>underlined</u> in the transcript. It may help students if you explain *some* of these beforehand. The answers are in **bold**.)

Answers

1	true	2	true	3	false, it is grown outside	4	true
5	false, he was a record producer	6	true			7	true
8	false, they leave with optimistic messages						

Transcript 3 minutes 40 seconds

Presenter: Listen to the interview with Sue Hill.

Sue: My name is Sue Hill and I'm the artistic director at the Eden Project in Cornwall.

Interviewer: And what does that involve?

Sue: It involves match-making artists to projects. So…er…the…the Project…the Eden Project took a very…um… interesting decision when it started to de…<u>devise</u> its <u>exhibits</u>. It decided to use artists to make the exhibits. Um…and I think this is a…this was a great decision because Cornwall especially has a…has a wonderful artistic <u>community</u> here, lots of really great artists. And so I work **with the artists to develop…um…ideas for…for exhibits to go into the project, to tell some of the plant stories there**.

Interviewer: Can you explain what the Eden Project is?

Sue: It's a global garden. What we've got there is two enormous greenhouses, the biggest in the world **one of which houses a tropical rainforest**, and the other houses…um…a display of plants from…from Mediterranean climates. Um…and we also have a huge outdoor landscape which is set in the Cornish climate, which is very mild and…um…friendly to plants, so **we grow some wonderful things outdoors as well: like tea plantations**, and fields of <u>sunflower</u> and <u>lavender</u>. The tea plant is a kind of <u>camellia</u> so it grows beautifully in Cornish soil.

Interviewer: But that's fantastic, isn't it?

Sue: Mm. Oh it's brilliant, yes. It's really amazing and it's one of the things that people . . . It takes people by surprise, and…and they find <u>enchanting</u>. You can go into the…into the…into the…er… rainforest at the Eden Project and **you can see cocoa trees and you can see…um…er…sugar…<u>sugar cane</u>**. And all these wonderful plants, we…we cons…we eat these things every day of our lives and…you…because you buy them in a <u>packet</u> in the supermarket you don't think about where they've come from or what they look like in their original state.

Interviewer: So when did the idea, when did Tim S…um…Tim Smit get the idea for . . . ?

Sue: For the project?

Interviewer: For the project.

Sue: His <u>background</u> was a music producer, he'd never had anything to do with plants in his life. **He'd been a record producer in London.**

Interviewer: Pop music?

Sue: Yeah, pop music. He…he'd become interested in the **<u>intimacy</u> of the relationship between plants and people**. It had never <u>occurred</u> to him before in his life and <u>it hit him</u> just what a powerful thing it was. We eat them, we drink them, we <u>perfume</u> ourselves with them, we take them as medicine, um…we build houses with them. You know, they are…they feature in every aspect of our daily lives. At…you know, by the time you've had breakfast you've consumed plants from every continent.

One day Tim was…was…driving home to Cornwall as the sun was setting and thought, 'This is it. What a dramatic place to…to put this exhibition and to…um…<u>interpret</u> these ideas'. It just so happened that he had this idea at the point when **the Millennium Commission…um…was looking for 'Landmark Projects' to mark the…the change of the millennium**. And so it became…it became reality.

Interviewer: That's fantastic.

Sue: It's tremendous. I think one of the things we felt very strongly is it was really important that we didn't make anybody feel <u>guilty</u>. If you really want people to look at the choices in their daily lives in a positive way, then **you have to give them**

positive, optimistic messages. And so wherever possible, we c…we try and showcase gr…good practice. And…er…no…er…nowhere do we tell people what to think. Rather than saying, 'This is how that, you know, this is how things are,' the kind of tone of the place is, 'We think this is really interesting, what do you think?' And we're kind of inviting people to make their own minds up about things rather than saying: 'This is wrong' or 'This is right'.

Comparing

Writing

1 👥 It's true, try it!

2 👥 Ask the pairs to share their ideas with the rest of the class at the end.

3 ✎ Model version

> Have you ever written a composition on a computer? It's so much easier than writing on paper, especially in a foreign language. You wish you could do all your writing this way – especially exams and tests. It's satisfying. It's convenient. You can make corrections and improvements as you go along. Using a keyboard takes a while to learn, but once you've learnt how, it's a skill you can use all your life. With a computer, you get the urge to write e-mails to all your friends. So much more fun than writing compositions. It makes you want to go on and on, adding new ideas whenever you think of them. You can write to your friend in Australia and a few minutes later you can read your friend's reply. Computers are more powerful than pens – and they have made the world smaller.

Follow-up questions

Speaking

1 🔊 👥 Pause the recording for the students to discuss possible questions. The problem with 'Yes/No' questions is that they can just be answered with 'Yes' or 'No'. Instead, Brian could have asked: 'What did you enjoy most?' and 'Why did you go on Sunday?'

🔊 Julie's techniques make Kevin say more – and in the end he becomes quite eloquent.

Transcript 1 minute

Presenter: Listen to two conversations. First Brian is talking to Kevin.

Brian:	Did you go to the zoo?
Kevin:	Yes.
Brian:	And did you enjoy it?
Kevin:	Mm.
Brian:	Did you go on Sunday?
Kevin:	Yeah.
Brian:	And…oh…did you . . .

Presenter: Now Julie is talking to Kevin.

Julie:	Did you go to the zoo?
Kevin:	Yes.

Julie:	Tell me about it, what did you enjoy?
Kevin:	Oh, well, we got there early to beat the crowds and we really enjoyed seeing all the animals and so on.
Julie:	Which animals did you like best?
Kevin:	Oh, I think the penguins were wonderful.
Julie:	Wonderful? Why?
Kevin:	Well, you can see them from below, swimming in their lake, and . . .

2 ◀» The phrases for repetition are in **bold**. There is a pause after each of these.

Transcript 1 minute

Presenter:	Listen to this conversation and repeat the phrases which are printed on the right in your book.

Woman:	Did you have a good trip?
1st man:	Yes.
Woman:	**Tell me about it.**
2nd man:	**What was good about it?**
1st man:	Well, we . . .

Woman:	Did the trip take a long time?
1st man:	Yes.
Woman:	**How long exactly did it take?**
2nd man:	**Why did it take so long?**
1st man:	Well, you see . . .

Woman:	Were you alone?
1st man:	No.
Woman:	**Who went with you?**
2nd man:	**How many people were with you?**
1st man:	Well, there were . . .

Woman:	Did you arrive on time?
1st man:	No.
Woman:	**When exactly did you arrive?**
2nd man:	**Why were you late?**
1st man:	Well, the reason was . . .

3 ▟▟ The questions in Activities 9 and 28 lead to a discussion about zoos, animals, gardens and living in the country. Students should use follow-up questions to persuade each other to expand on their answers.

15 Free time

15A Hobbies and games
15B Sports and activities

The aims of **15A** and **15B** are:

- to encourage students to talk about their favourite hobbies, games, sports and leisure activities
- to revise the past perfect
- to recognize words that are 'false friends' in English and their own language
- to practise writing a story
- to practise using emphasis in conversation

> *Every game ever invented by mankind, is a way of making things hard for the fun of it!* – John Anthony Ciardi
>
> *Men forget everything; women remember everything. That's why men need instant replays in sports. They've already forgotten what happened.* – Rita Rudner
>
> *A hot dog at the ball park is better than steak at the Ritz.* – Humphrey Bogart
>
> *All work and no play makes Jack a dull boy.* – English proverb

15A Hobbies and games

So much to do, so little time!   Speaking and vocabulary

There is a lot of vocabulary in these three sections, but no vocabulary exercise. Encourage everyone to highlight the words they want to remember, and use dictionaries when necessary.

1 👥 Many people are 'collectors' without realizing it.

2 👥 then 👥+👥 At the end, combine the pairs for them to compare ideas.

3 👥 Change partners for this. The (not-too-serious) evaluation of the scores is in **Part 1** of **Activity 27**.

Part 2 of Activity 27 then gives an extra task for the students to do: categorize the sports in the list.

Suggested answers

Outdoor sports: football   golf   running   sailing   ski-ing   snowboarding   surfing   swimming   tennis   walking   windsurfing

Popular spectator sports: basketball   cycling   football   golf   gymnastics   skating   ski-ing   swimming   tennis

All-year-round sports: – these depend on the climate in your country, but you do need snow to snowboard and ski.

Solo sports: cycling   dancing   golf   gymnastics   running   sailing   skating   ski-ing   snowboarding   surfing   swimming   tennis   walking   windsurfing   working out

Competitive sports – all *except*:   aerobics   dancing   Frisbee   working out

Indoor sports: aerobics   basketball   dancing   gymnastics   skating   swimming   working out

Summer-only sports – these depend on the climate in your country! (In the UK the only summer-only sport is cricket.)

Team sports: basketball   football   volleyball

Ball games: basketball   football   golf   tennis   volleyball

Not really sports at all: aerobics?   dancing?   Frisbee?   working out?

Past perfect

Typical mistakes

They already finished their meal before I arrived.
By the time she had arrived we finished our meal.
She told me that she never met Bill before.

1 If possible students should have read the Grammar reference section before the lesson.

2 👥 **Answers**

2 she had always wanted to meet him.
3 they had arranged to meet on Friday.
4 she had arrived early.
5 she had waited for over an hour.
6 he had never shown up.

3 👥 **Answers**

1 It was my first visit to a football match. I **had** never **attended** one before. Well, I **had watched** my brother play at school, but that doesn't count. We **had bought** our tickets in advance, to make sure we **got** good seats. Before half time our team **had** already **scored** a goal. But by the end of the match the other side **had equalized** and just before the final whistle **blew**, they **got** another goal. We all **felt** very disappointed.

2 They **had** already **finished** their meal by the time I **arrived**. They **had eaten** all the food and **hadn't** even **left** me any bread. I **felt** pretty cross because this **had happened** the previous time I **got** home late and I **didn't expect** that it would happen again!

'False friends'

1 👥 Quite a few of these pairs may not be false friends for your students. Encourage the use of dictionaries while the students are doing this.

Some answers (Just to show what students might come up with.)

An **agenda** is the programme for a meeting. A **notebook** is a little book to make notes in. (A **diary** is a little book with dates in.)

To **assist** means to help. To **attend** means to be present at a meeting or performance.

A **conference** is a gathering of people who listen to lectures and attend seminars. A **lecture** is one person giving a speech to a group of people, usually students.

To **control** is to be in charge of something and make people do what you tell them to. To **check** is to make sure something is correct. (At passport control, an immigration officer will check your passport.)

To **cry** is to shed tears. To **shout** is to speak very loudly.
etc.

2 👥 It's worth doing some research here to find out what your students may find difficult.

For example, some Greek students find these words confusing:

air · wind   fortune · storm   sympathize · like
woman · wife   finger · toe

And some German students find these words confusing:

receive · become   mean · think   will · want   when · if   walk · go
handy · mobile phone

(See *Learner English* by Michael Swan and Bernard Smith, Cambridge University Press, for more information about different nationalities.)

15B Sports and activities

Arthur Melin

Reading

1 You could ask students to fill in the chart in pairs.

Answers

	first popular	number sold	invented by
Frisbee	1958	100 million	Fred Morrison
Superball	1960s	20 million	Norman Stingley
Hula-Hoop	summer 1958	40 million	Melin and Knerr
Instant Fish	never	none	Melin

2 **Answers**

¶2   pal
¶3   craze   royalties
¶5   prototype
¶6   nutty   bounced

Writing a story

Writing

1 ✏ ▟▟ then ▟▟ + ▟▟ You may prefer students to finish off their improvements as homework, then compare them in the next lesson.

Model versions

> We were driving along a very quiet road in the middle of winter when our car started making a very strange noise and then the engine coughed and stopped. We tried and tried to restart the engine, but it was no good. It was then that we realized we had run out of petrol. We didn't know what to do. There was no signal on my mobile and there was no traffic on that road.
>
> We waited and waited for another car to come along, and it was getting darker and darker. In the end, after we had waited for two hours, we saw headlights approaching. We stood in the road waving for the driver to stop, but he drove right past us. Then he braked and stopped and reversed back to where we were standing. We were so happy to be rescued. We left our car by the side of the road, until the next morning, when we returned with a full can of petrol.

Free time

The first time Bob and Annie met was on a blind date. This first date was not a great success and they really didn't get on, so they decided not to see each other again. But after a few days they had second thoughts and decided to give it another try and go out together again. This time it was even worse: they had a blazing row and ended up screaming at each other all evening.

Some months later they met again by chance and got on really well. They decided to start going out regularly. It was only later that they realized they were in love. They got married and now they have seven children.

They are still married, and still in love.

It was the very first time I had played football. My friend's team was a player short so he persuaded me to take part and lent me some boots. It was a very strange experience, because I didn't really know the rules, but I managed to play on till it was nearly the end of the match without making too much of a fool of myself.

Then one minute before the final whistle, I was standing near our opponents' goal. The ball came flying in the air towards me and it hit me on the head. I fell to the ground, but the ball went straight into the net. We won the match and it was me who had scored the winning goal! I haven't played again since then. I might not be so lucky again!

2 ✎ Only sports-minded students should write about a sporting experience.

Emphasis   Speaking

1 ◀)) **Transcript** (Emphasized words are in **bold**.) 40 seconds

Presenter: Listen to the conversations and underline the underline the words that are emphasized.

Man: Was the match exciting?
Woman: Exciting? Yes, it was **very** exciting! I've **never** seen such an exciting match!

Woman: Was it a romantic movie?
Man: Wow, yes. It was **really** romantic! I've never **seen** such a romantic movie!

Man: Was there enough food?
Woman: Oh, yes! There was **loads** of food! There was so much food that we **all** ate **far** too much!

2 ◀)) **Play the recording. There is a pause after each line for the students to practise their pronunciation.**

Transcript (50 seconds)

Presenter: Now practise saying the answers.

Man: Was the match exciting?
Woman: Exciting? Yes, it was very exciting! I've never seen such an exciting match.

Woman: Was it a romantic movie?

Man: Wow, yes. It was really romantic! I've never seen such a romantic movie!

Man: Was there enough food?

Woman: Oh, yes! There was loads of food! There was so much food that we all ate far too much

3 🏛 **Some suggested answers**

Yes, we had lots of fun.

Yes, he has loads of money.

Yes, we have plenty of money.

Yes, it was a **very** good book.

11–15 Revision

Topic vocabulary

Answers

11 Words from Unit 11

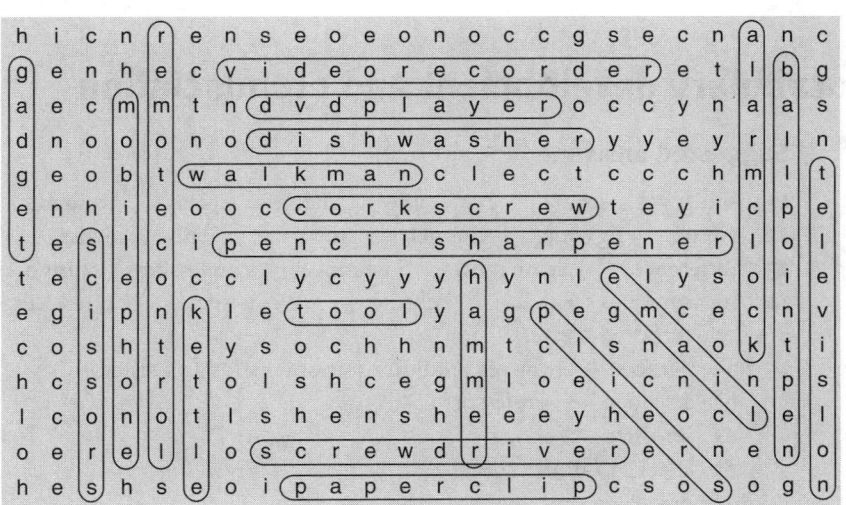

13–14 Words from Units 13 and 14

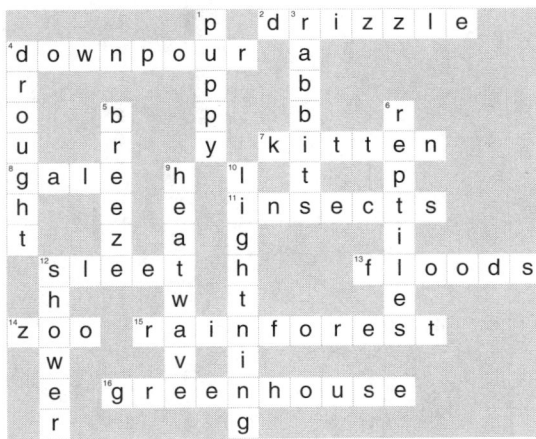

Grammar review

A Suggested answers

11 was invented   is used   are compressed   be downloaded
12 had   might/would   gave   wouldn't   'd/would   could   'd/would
    'd/would spend   won't / isn't going to   'll/will   is   might/will
13 would be / was going to be   if it would / if it might / if it was going to   she wanted to
    wouldn't/didn't
14 looked   saw/realized   was   were playing   were having   walked/went
    was trying   went   gave   drove
15 had driven / drove   stopped   reversed   got   went   was   opened
    started   drove   had   forgotten   had left

B Suggested answers

11 has never been cleaned
12 had more time I'd / I would
13 if someone would clean it if she paid
14 was still cleaning
15 pay me after I'd / I had cleaned

Vocabulary development and pronunciation

Suggested answers

11 hungry   sunny   preferable   helpful/helpless   accidental
12 Greek   Egyptian   French   Spanish   Irish   Swiss
13 difference   explanation   insurance   carelessness   innocence   enjoyment
14 maximum   Square   February   Wednesday   United Kingdom   approximately
    one hundred metres
15 a) parents   relatives/relations *or* mother's/father's sisters
    b) attended   professor   lecture
    c) sensitive   shout
    d) checked / didn't check
(**Note:** there are several possible answers in **15**.)

16 Good health

16A Staying well
16B Keeping fit

The aims of **16A** and **16B** are:

- to encourage students to talk about their experiences of medical matters and keeping fit and healthy
- to revise articles and quantifiers
- to practise word-stress
- to practise giving advice in writing and speaking

Never go to a doctor whose office plants have died. – Erma Louise Bombeck
An apple a day keeps the doctor away. – English proverb
Early to bed and early to rise makes a man healthy, wealthy and wise. – English proverb

16A Staying well

Good health

Speaking and vocabulary

1 Bear in mind that some of your students may be unduly sensitive about health matters. Ask the pairs to share their best ideas. For example:

- What exactly are you doing?
- How will this help you to stay fit and healthy?
- This looks a bit dangerous to me. Is it?

- You ought to take more exercise.
- Using a remote control isn't very good exercise.
- Eating popcorn will make you fat.

2 Answers

1 appointment   dentist
2 cough   sneeze   headache   sick
3 injections/immunizations   diseases   tablets
4 patient
5 injured   ambulance
6 pain

3 Some suggested answers

red zone	shoulders	head	scalp	ears	nose	neck	chest	eyes
	cheeks	armpits					
yellow zone	wrist	thumb	index finger	palm	forearm	hips	waist
	bottom	thighs					
blue zone	knee	ankle	heel	big toe	sole	instep	

4 👥 Expand the pairs into groups (or reassemble the whole class) for them to share their best ideas.

Just a few suggested answers

I'd lie down.
I'd loosen their clothes and wait till they came round.
I'd read a book till I fell asleep.
I'd make sure I had plenty of tissues.
I'd stay in bed till I felt a bit better.

I'd take an aspirin.
I'd go to hospital. / I'd have to keep my arm in a sling.
I'd go to the doctor.
I'd avoid walking too much.
I'd start taking some gentle exercise.

Articles and quantifiers – 2

Grammar practice

Typical mistakes
See **3** in the Student's Book.

1 Ask students to read this before the class.

2 👥 **Suggested answers**

The police means the police in general, *a police officer* is one particular policeman or policewoman.
A country is the same as a nation, *the country* is the area away from towns or cities.
I'd like an apple means one apple, but not a particular one.
I'd like some apples means 'I would like more than one apple, but I don't mind which in particular'.
I like apples means that I like apples in general.

NOTE: *I'd like **the** apple* means a particular (already shown or offered) apple:
   There's a pear and an apple – which would you like?
   — I'd like the apple.

We went to the island *by sea* means travelling by boat, *by the sea* means near or beside the sea.
A cold is a virus, *the cold* means low air temperature.

3 👥 **Answers**

1 I have **a** problem, can you give me **some** advice, please?
2 ~~The~~ New cars cost more than second-hand ones.
   or **A** new car costs more than a second-hand one.
3 If you have **a** high temperature, you'd better go to ~~the~~ bed.
4 To become **a** doctor you have to study ~~the~~ medicine.
5 Do you go to school by ~~the~~ bus or on ~~the~~ foot?
6 If you have **a** headache take **an** aspirin.

4 👥 **Answers** (Ø = no article)

1 Normally I love **Ø** music, but I really don't like **the** music she plays.
2 I usually drink **Ø** water with **Ø** meals, but I prefer **the** water you get in **Ø** bottles to **the** water you get from **the/a** tap.
3 He wanted to be **a** dentist but he didn't have **the** right qualifications to get onto **the** course.
4 **The** best way to stay in **Ø** good health is to take plenty of **Ø** exercise and eat **Ø** healthy food. And don't smoke **Ø** cigarettes. **Ø** Yoga is more relaxing than **Ø** aerobics and helps to reduce **Ø** stress.
5 **The** United States is on **the** other side of **the** Atlantic from **Ø** Europe.
   The state of **Ø** California is in **the** West on **the** Pacific Coast.

Stréssing the corréct sýllable

1 🔊 The words are recorded. Ask everyone to try marking the stresses in pencil *before* they hear the recording (30 seconds).

Answers

<u>á</u>ctually   <u>é</u>xcellent   <u>má</u>rvellous   <u>mó</u>dern   <u>nór</u>mally   oc<u>cá</u>sionally   par<u>tí</u>cularly   <u>pró</u>bably   un<u>fór</u>tunately

2 👥 Answers in **Activity 20**.

3 👥 Answers in **Activity 44**. Saying the months in reverse order is quite hard and focuses the students' attention on the word-stress.

4 👥 **Some suggested words**

page 75   témperature   cigaréttes
page 73   árgument   evéntually   ignítion   enjóyable   Swítzerland
page 72   depártment   ínstitute

At the end

Many students have difficulty using the right word-stress with numbers. To practise this, write up these numbers and ask the class to say them aloud:

7	11	13	14	15
30	31	32		
40	41	47		
50	51	57		

👥 Now put the class in pairs and ask them to take turns to say all the numbers from 57 down to 7 in descending order, with one doing the even numbers and the other the odd numbers.

16B Keeping fit

At the gym

1 👥 This vocabulary exercise introduces some of the more difficult words the speakers will use. The speakers are Andy and Rachel, who we heard in **4B** talking about their memories of school.

Answers

rewards · satisfying advantages
hurdles · difficulties
firm · strict
like-minded people · people who have the same attitude
worn out · tired
down side · disadvantage
get my heart rate up · make my heart beat faster
vitamin supplements · tablets to give you extra vitamins

② 🔊 Answers (Corrections are <u>underlined</u>)

1 Andy finds that his professional attitude makes it <u>easier</u> for clients.
2 Andy <u>doesn't</u> always speak softly to his clients.
3 Andy <u>meets lots of</u> healthy people during his work.
4 It takes <u>four</u> weeks for people to feel the effects of their training.
5 Andy says there is <u>no</u> disadvantage to keeping fit.
6 Rachel <u>didn't find</u> yoga a very effective way of keeping fit.
7 She goes to the gym <u>three times</u> a week and spends <u>one hour</u> there.
8 <u>Because</u> she has a fitness instructor she <u>doesn't feel</u> bored at the gym.
9 Rachel <u>doesn't always</u> feel like a session at the gym.
10 Andy <u>sometimes</u> shouts at Rachel. (She says 'all the time' but that's a joke.)

Transcript (Answers are in **bold**.) 4 minutes

Presenter: Listen to Andy and Rachel. First Andy.

Andy: My name's Andrew Parsons, and I'm a personal fitness instructor.
Interviewer: And what sort of a relationship do you have with your clients?
Andy: I think…um…you've got to come across as a professional. Um…they've got to be able to get something from you, um…you've got to be in a position to actually encourage them to make progress and…and…and let them see some rewards. **So I suppose keeping a quite a kind of professional attitude towards it makes it easier for me and easier for them.**
Interviewer: And do you find that you have to bully them sometimes?
Andy: Not at all, but part of…um…part of fitness…or one of…one of the hurdles of getting over fitness is…um…you know, pushing yourself just that little bit harder. So, you know, sometimes **you do have to encourage them**…you know… some…some, **you know, a loud voice helps.**
Interviewer: Kind but firm.
Andy: 'Kind but firm' is…er…one way of putting it.
Interviewer: And what do you most enjoy about it?
Andy: I think **it's a healthy environment, a healthy life-style**. I enjoy doing the physical side, the physical…er…aspect of working in that industry's…er…it's fun, and you're surrounded by fun and like-minded people. So…and it's nice to see…er…people achieving something, which is, you know, it's a good reward for me.
Interviewer: And do you…have you ch…seen…um…a mental attitude in people change as they get fitter?
Andy: 'Course they do because you get a kind of zest for life, you get your fitness back, you start recognizing that you're not so…er…worn out and one of the…one of the first things you notice as you start to get fitter, and normally we're talking about, you know, **28 days before you see real results from someone**. Um…your fitness comes back and you start being able to do things or not noticing that you're getting tired. I think another thing with fitness is…er…people do recognize that they have actually…have more energy and the more fitness you do the more energy you have, so it's…er…you know, it's…it's completely beneficial, **there's no down side**.

Presenter: Now let's hear from Rachel.

Rachel: My name's Rachel Babington, and I work in public relations for a kids' TV channel.
Interviewer: And what…er…what d…why did you start coming to the gym?
Rachel: Well, really I…I was quite interested in…um…yoga and that's what got me started and then I realized that although that was lovely, **it wasn't really getting me fit** and getting my heart rate up.
Interviewer: So was it for a…sort of health reasons, do you think?

Rachel:	Yes, really to try and stay trim and…um…stay healthy, I suppose.
Interviewer:	And what do you do on a typical visit?
Rachel:	Um…well, I usually use the machine, so I'll do a bit of running, try and get my heart rate up, um…stretching and then go on to weights.
Interviewer:	And how long do you spend doing this?
Rachel:	**I try and spend an hour each time I go, three times a week.**
Interviewer:	And what do you most enjoy about going to the gym?
Rachel:	Well, I guess it's that sense of well-being an…and achievement and feeling you…er…er…and seeing your fitness levels going up. Um…and I guess that's **the good thing about having a fitness instructor, that you never get bored,** they keep introducing new ways of…of keeping fit and…and pushing you, really.
Interviewer:	What else do you do to stay healthy?
Rachel:	Um…well, I…I eat healthily, and I try and watch what I drink, um…and I take vitamin supplements, but I'm not, you know, fanatical about it.
Interviewer:	And why do you think people should keep fit?
Rachel:	I suppose it's…I suppose the main reason is…is for health, but I think it can be really fun and I think doing regular exercise gives you a self-confidence an…and that's a good thing too.
Interviewer:	Do you ever do…have a personal fitness…er…session that you really don't want to do and you'd much rather be…um…in the jacuzzi or having a sauna or something?
Rachel:	**Yes, frequently!** Haha.
Interviewer:	Haha. Does…does Andy, your trainer, ever have to shout at you?
Rachel:	**All the time!** He's very disciplined. It's his army background.
Interviewer:	Yes, well, still, that's quite sort of fun, I suppose, isn't it?
Rachel:	Oh yes!

Giving advice

Speaking and writing

1 👥 More ideas might be: 'Travel by bike' and 'Don't overeat' and 'Take up swimming'.

2 🔊 The recording lasts 40 seconds with pauses for repetition.

3 👥 **Answers**

1   fingers   hands   chest   hands   arms   head

2   arms/hands   arms   elbows   head

3   arms   arms/hands

4 👥 In **Activities 10** and **30** each student has a problem which the exercises in the partner's **Activity** can help with.
They have to explain the exercises to each other.

5 👥 Upset? Angry? Amused? What a rude friend!

Model version

Dear Max,

I'm sorry to hear you've been feeling unwell. I hope you don't mind me saying this, but I think it might be because you don't take enough exercise. Have you considered this? Eating too much makes any person put on weight so they don't look their best. In particular, foods like ice cream, hamburgers and pizzas are quite unhealthy. All the experts agree that healthy food is better for you, particularly fruit and vegetables. I know you love fruit, so you should eat more of it. And salads are good too.

Another idea might be to do what I did: join a gym. I thought it would be difficult to keep going regularly, but now I go at the same time each day, so it's easy to keep it up.

Or, how about swimming? That's good because you can start with gentle exercise and gradually build up your speed and distance.

So, Max, I hope you'll take my advice. You won't regret it!

Love,
Sophie

17 Puzzles and problems

17A How strange!
17B Solving problems

The aims of **17A** and **17B** are:

- to encourage students to use English together when trying to solve puzzles and problems (and to have fun whilst doing this!)
- to revise second conditionals
- to practise collocations with *make*, *take* and *do*
- to encourage students to correct their own mistakes when proof-reading their work
- to practise repetition and clarification in conversation

Every problem has a gift for you in its hands. – Richard David Bach
I think the next best thing to solving a problem is finding some humour in it. – Frank A. Clark
You often get a better hold upon a problem by going away from it for a time and dismissing it from your mind altogether. – Frank H. Crane
A problem is a chance for you to do your best. – Duke Ellington
Life is a continuous exercise in creative problem-solving. – Michael J. Gelb
You won't find a solution by saying there is no problem. – William Rotsler
A positive attitude may not solve all your problems, but it will annoy enough people to make it worth the effort.
I don't have a solution but I admire the problem.

17A How strange!

Puzzling it out

1 👥 There are no correct answers!

2 👥 Ask the class which they found hardest to read and why.

Answers

a Some puzzles are much harder to solve than others.
b An optical illusion confuses the brain so that you can't trust your eyes.
c I find it very hard to solve a puzzle that has numbers in it.

3 👥 Allow plenty of time for this. The purpose of the activity is to stimulate conversation, using problem-solving skills. Although, of course, there are correct solutions, it's using English that's the focus.

Answers

a The next two numbers in the sequence are **31** and **30**:
   January has 31 days   February usually has 28 days   March has 31 days
   April has 30 days   **May** has **31** days   **June** has **30** days

b The next two letters in the sequence are **E** and **N**:
   One   Two   Three   Four   Five   Six   Seven   Eight   Nine

c The next two letters in the sequence are **T** and **R**:
   JanuarY   FebruarY   MarcH   ApriL   MaY   JunE   JulY
   AugusT   SeptembeR

d The letter **e**: minut**e**, w**ee**k, y**e**ar

e 1 + 2 + 3 + 4 + 5 + 6 + 7 + 8 + 9 + 10 + 11 + 12 + 1 + 2 + 3 + 4 + 5 + 6 + 7 + 8 + 9 + 10 + 11 + 12 = **156 times**

f 1 = A   2 = B   3 = C   . . .   26 = Z
   some puzzles are harder than others

g 1 = A   2 = E   3 = I   4 = O   5 = U
   WELLDONE YOUHAVEFINISHEDTHESEPUZZLES

4 👥 + 👥 Allow plenty of time for comparing answers, so that those that know can explain to those that don't. Remind everyone that the purpose of all this is to give them ideas to share in English.

If... sentences – 2

Typical mistakes
See **3** in the Student's Book.

1 To save time ask students to read this before they come to class, if possible.

2 👥 **Suggested answers**

1 *If I knew the answer I would tell you.* = I don't know the answer, so I can't tell you. (now)
   If I had known the answer I would have told you. = I didn't know the answer, so I couldn't tell you (in the past).

2 *What would you do if the lights went out?* = The lights are unlikely to go out, but just suppose they did . . .
What will you do if the lights go out? = The lights are likely to go out. If they do, what will you do?

3 *If we run out of money what can we do?* = It is likely that we will run out of money.
If we ran out of money what could we do? = It is not likely that we will run out of money.

3 👥 **Answers** (Corrections are <u>underlined</u>.)

1 I would have phoned her if I <u>had</u> known her number.

2 What would you have done if you <u>had</u> missed the last bus home yesterday?

3 If I <u>had been</u> born in England, I'd have learnt English as a child.

4 I <u>wouldn't/couldn't have solved</u> the problem unless <u>I'd had / I had had</u> some help.

4 👥 **Suggested answers**

2 But if I had had / if I'd had enough money I could have bought the CD.

3 But if my computer hadn't crashed, I wouldn't have lost all my work.

4 But we wouldn't have lost our way if we'd had / we had had a map.

5 But if we had stayed / we'd stayed at home we wouldn't have got soaking wet.

6 But he wouldn't have felt so sick if he hadn't eaten so much ice cream.

Make, take and *do*   Vocabulary development

1 👥 **Answers**

1 did   made   **2** took/did   **3** took *or* had   did   **4** made   did
5 did   made   **6** made   made

2 👥 **Answers**

make	~~a rest~~	**do**	~~a noise~~	**take**	~~a promise~~
	~~the washing-up~~		~~a photo~~		~~an appointment~~
	+		+		+
	an appointment		the washing-up		a photo
	a promise				a rest
	a noise				

3 ✏️ 👥 then 👥👥 Combine the pairs into groups for them to show each other their sentences.

At the end

If there's time, here are two more puzzles for the whole class to try:

> You are a bus driver. At the first stop, four people get on. At the second stop, eight more people get on. At the third stop, two people get off, and at the last stop, everyone gets off. The question is: What colour are the bus driver's eyes?

(You are the bus driver, so the answer is the colour of your own eyes.)

> You and a friend are planning to go hiking separately and meet at a lake neither of you has ever been to before. The lake is in a hilly area, with plenty of streams and trees. You're sure you can find the lake, and walk around it if necessary, but visibility might be poor. Where should you arrange to meet to be sure of finding each other?

(Lakes may have many inflows, but only one outflow. Arrange to meet at the lake's outflow. If you don't think you can find a place to cross the outflowing stream, agree to meet on the true left bank of the outflow [true left = left bank when facing downstream].)

17B Solving problems

Stretch your brain

1 To start off, remind everyone that the idea is to use *English* to solve the problems together. There are no prizes for the first to finish. If an early problem seems insoluble, students should move on to the next and come back to it later if they have time.

2 It's important to allow plenty of time for comparing answers. This gives everyone a chance to *explain* their reasons.

At the end, even if students ask you to tell them the answers, it's better for members of the class who know to tell the others.

Answers

A   Take the second glass, pour its contents into the fifth glass, then replace it.

B   In any book, page 75 is a right-hand page and page 76 is a left-hand page. There is no space between them to hide anything.

C   The word 'wrong'

D   It doesn't contain a single 'e', which is the most frequent letter in English.

E   First fill up the three-litre jug and pour the water into the five-litre bottle. Then fill the jug again and fill the bottle to the top. The remaining water in the jug is one litre.

F   'One word' is the correct answer.

G   10 times

H   One thousand

I   Three sweaters

Spoting mistakes – 1

1 Did the students spot the mistake in the title?

Answers (The corrections are underlined. Students need to learn to find mistakes in their own work. This is especially important in an exam.)

You find shelter in a mountain hut on a windy night. You need to light a fire to get warm. There is plenty of wood, but only one match, one piece of newspaper and one candle. What do you light first?

– spelling mistakes

A woman was asleep in a hotel. In the middle of the night she woke up and couldn't go back to sleep. She picked up the phone and made a phone call. She hung up and went to sleep again. Who did she call and why?

– grammar mistakes

A town has only two hair salons. One has a broken mirror, dirty floor covered in hair, torn magazines and the hairdresser has a terrible haircut. The other has a new mirror, clean floor, new magazines and a hairdresser with a great haircut. Where would you go and why?

– punctuation mistakes

Puzzles and problems

Last week I was able to turn the bedroom light off and get into bed before the room was <u>in</u> darkness. The bed and the light <u>switch</u> are two metres <u>apart</u>. Can you <u>guess/work out</u> how I did this?

– vocabulary mistakes

2 This should be done together. At the end, discuss the outcome: what were the most 'popular' types of mistakes?

Repetition and clarification

Speaking

1 The conversation is the explanation of the second puzzle in **1**. The phrases that were used are in **bold** in the transcript.

Transcript 1 minute

Presenter: Listen to the conversation and tick the phrases that are used.

Woman: No, you see the woman was, you know, sort of asleep . . .

Man: **I'm sorry, I didn't catch what you said.**

Woman: She was asleep. OK?

Man: Oh, yes, asleep. OK.

Woman: And she got woken up by the snoring . . .

Man: **Sorry, I don't quite understand.**

Woman: Um…**let me put it another way:** there was a man snoring, you know, making a noise like this (*snore*) while he was sleeping.

Man: Oh, I see. Right, but **I don't quite follow.** Where was the snoring man?

Woman: In the room next door.

Man: Oh, right. And the walls were thin?

Woman: That's right. So she phoned the room next door.

Man: **I'm not with you.**

Woman: Well, you see, the phone ringing woke the snoring man up, so she was able to go back to sleep.

Man: Oh, I see. Haha!

2 The phrases are recorded (1 minute).

3 If students live in a very small place, with no well-known buildings, they might prefer to talk about a large city they know.

At the end

If there's time, use the extra puzzles at the end of **17A**, if you didn't do them earlier.

18 The future

18A Looking ahead
18B Hopes and ambitions

The aims of 18A and 18B are:

- to encourage students to talk about the future and their ambitions
- to revise the use of *for* and *since*, and the present perfect simple and continuous
- to look at some of the differences between British and American English vocabulary
- to practise writing about advantages and disadvantages (pros and cons)
- to practise using the telephone

> *The best thing about the future is that it comes one day at a time.* – Abraham Lincoln
> *There is always one moment in childhood when the door opens and lets the future in.* – Graham Greene
> *The future starts today, not tomorrow.* – Pope John Paul II
> *When it comes to the future, there are three kinds of people: those who let it happen, those who make it happen, and those who wonder what happened.*
> *Learn from the past, watch the present, and create the future.*
> *The future belongs to those who prepare for it today.*
> *The future belongs to those who dare.*

18A Looking ahead

The 21st century

Speaking and vocabulary

1 Maybe brainstorm some ideas and write them on the board, to start everyone off:

dishwasher, remote control, vacuum cleaner, food processor, mobile phone, photocopier, etc.

2 **Answers**

1	likelihood	forecast	**2**	predict	bring	**3**	hope/expect	career
4	expect	saw it coming	**5**	ambition	optimistic	**6**	looking forward to

3 **Answers**
1 *Al's definitely going to Austria.*
4 *Bob may not go to Belgium.*
3 *Carl might just possibly go to Cambridge.*
2 *Nina may go to New Zealand.*
6 *Olive's very unlikely to go to Oxford.*
5 *Pam probably won't go to Panama.*

4 In case anyone asks you for suitable places, here are some suggestions:

Australia   Berlin   Crete   the Dominican Republic   Egypt   Finland   Greece
Honduras   India   Jerusalem   Kazakhstan   Lima   Manchester

Norwich   Oslo   Puerto Rico   Queensland   Russia   Switzerland   Tokyo
Ukraine   Vietnam   Washington   Xylofagou (a small town in Cyprus!)
Yemen   Zimbabwe

At the end

Ask everyone to make a list of some things that might happen or machines that might be invented in the next ten years, including a few unlikely ones. Then arrange the students into groups so that they can compare their lists and say how likely each invention is.

For and *since*

Typical mistakes

See **3** in the Student's Book.

1 Ask your students to read this section before coming to class. This section also practises the present perfect continuous and the present perfect simple.

2 👥 **Suggested answers**

She has lived there for four years. = She still lives there now.

She lived there for four years. = She doesn't live there now.

I have been reading this book. = I have spent some time reading it (and I may not have finished it).

I have read this book. = I have read the whole book.

Someone has been drinking my milk. = There is some milk left but there isn't as much in the glass as there was.

Someone has drunk my milk. = There is no milk left: all my milk has been drunk.

3 👥 **Answers**

2 She has been studying in London for two years. / She studied in London for two years.

3 I haven't drunk milk for two years.

4 I have only read ten pages of the book so far.

4 👥 **Answers**

1	have you been studying	**2**	have you read
3	have seen	**4**	has visited
5	have been waiting here for	**6**	have been playing since
7	has been ringing has answered	**8**	have been discussing since

British and American English

1 👥 **Quite a few of these terms may be unknown to your students. Encourage them to highlight the new words they want to remember.**

Answers

biscuit · cookie   boot (of a car) · trunk   city centre · downtown   colleague · co-worker

CV · résumé   first floor · second floor   ground floor · first floor   fortnight · two weeks

holiday · vacation   public holiday · holiday   lift (in a building) · elevator

motorway · highway, freeway (also Interstate, expressway, etc.)   petrol · gas   sweets · candy

timetable · schedule   toilet · bathroom, restroom   trousers · pants

Answers

29/02/04	dialling code	post code
Summer Time	Monday to Friday	ten past six
pavement	underground/metro	windscreen
colour	centre	neighbour

At the end
You might like to mention some more equivalents. (The British term is first in each case.)

road surface · pavement   mean · stingy   nasty · mean   pedestrian crossing · crosswalk
cutlery · silverware   slip road · on ramp/off ramp   waistcoat · vest
teaching staff · faculty   state school · public school   football · soccer   maths · math

18B Hopes and ambitions

Five years from now . . .

Listening

1   **Pause the recording after each interview.**

Answers

	five years from now		
	work or uni	**free time**	**relationships**
Tony	start own graphic design company (with friends)	take up surfing spend more time snow-boarding	married – maybe a father
Amy	study languages	rock-climbing	make new friends, stay in touch with old friends
Daniel	sports teacher or fitness instructor	play the flute	stay friends with present friends – not get married
Sarah	no idea what work	do more painting	stay friends with everyone, make new friends

Transcript (Tricky words are underlined.)   3 minutes 20 seconds

Presenter: Listen to four people talking about their ambitions and what they hope the future will bring them.

Tony: My name's Tony. I'm…er…25 years old, and I currently work as a <u>graphic designer</u>, I…er…do designs for various web sites. At the moment I'm working for a…a small company in…er…London. In five years' time, what will I be doing? Er…<u>work-wise</u> I'm…I'm planning to start my own company with a couple of <u>mates</u>. Um…my free time, I really want to take up surfing, and…er…I <u>snow-board</u> and so…er…I want to spend more time doing that as well. Relationship-wise I will be a married man! My girlfriend and I got engaged last weekend, the wedding's this Christmas. Um…oh, I could even be a father by then! Haha!

Amy: I'm Amy, I'm 16, still at school. In five years' time, well, I'll be at university. I really want to go and study languages. And if I do I'll get to spend a year abroad, you know, as a teacher assistant in a school there, maybe in France or somewhere like that. That'd be brilliant. Um…in my free time, well, you know, I tried <u>rock-climbing</u> last summer and I really liked it. So hopefully I'm going to be able to do some more of that, maybe in the Alps if I get to France. Er…<u>relationship-wise</u>, well, I hope to make loads of new friends when I go to uni, and of course…like…stay in touch with all my good friends back here.

Daniel: My name's Daniel, and I'm 20, er…and I'm at university at the moment…er…studying sports. Um…in five years' time? Um…well, I imagine…um…I'll still be doing something involved with sports so I see myself probably getting a job as a sports teacher in a school. Or, if not that, then I'd quite like to become…um…a fitness instructor in a…in a leisure…leisure centre, something like that anyway. Um…in my free time…um…I'm quite musical…er…I play the flute, I play in the university orchestra at the moment, which is quite good fun. Um…and I hope to…I hope to keep it up. So I hope…I hope I'm still playing in the future. Um…as for relationships…um…well, there's a group of us who <u>hang out together</u> and…um…I think we'll still be friends in five years' time. Hope so…I hope so, anyway. Um…but by then I <u>reckon</u> that at least two of us'll be married. Not me though, no way! Haha!

Sarah: Hi, I'm Sarah and I'm 19. Um…currently I'm on my <u>gap year</u> before I start university, which will be next September. I'm working in a shop at the moment to earn some money…um…to go travelling. I'm going to get an <u>InterRail Pass</u> and…er…go by train all over Europe with a friend of mine. Um…in five years' time, oh, I haven't a clue what work I'll be doing. No idea whatsoever! Um…in my free time, well, I really loved art at school and I hope I'll be able to do more painting in my free time, er…not professionally though, not like Tony! So…um…and relationships, well, I don't even want to think about that. Just friends, I…I just want to stay friends with everyone…er…everyone I know now and…and make more friends in the future.

For and against

Writing

Almost everyone finds it hard to write a good 'discursive essay'. And doing it in a foreign language is even harder. Unfortunately, as with most writing skills, there are no helpful easy-to-follow rules on how to construct one. There are some phrases which can help to get people started (see **3** in the Student's Book), but really the only way to improve is to practise, and to receive guidance and encouragement in developing one's skills. This section encourages students to brainstorm and make notes and experiment. Half the battle for some students is coming up with ideas in the first place.

1 Students should brainstorm ideas, then compare ideas with another pair. Some extra advantages, and disadvantages, might be:

- If you have plans you can consider alternatives and make choices.
- Qualifications, such as exams, have to be planned ahead. You have to prepare for them if you want to pass.
- Your circumstances and attitudes may change over time.
- A rigid plan can control your life and prevent you from reacting to events.

2 At the end, ask the pairs to report their best ideas to the whole class.

3 Urge everyone to make notes before they write their composition. A list of pros and cons, arranged and then rearranged, not only helps you to think, it helps you to organize your writing.

Maybe ask the students to write sentences in class, using each of the phrases, before they write their composition. You might like to set a word limit for the composition, 150 words maybe.

Telephoning

1 👥 Most people get nervous when calling a stranger, especially in a foreign language. Do the members of the class feel different when using a mobile phone from when using a landline? Do they behave differently?

2 🔊 👥 There's a pause after each line for pronunciation practice.

Transcript 1 minute

Man:	Could I speak to Anne, please?
Woman:	She's not here. Can I take a message?
Man:	Could you ask her to phone me, please?
Woman:	Who's calling, please?
Man:	My name is Terry and my number is 5 . . . *(crackle crackle)*
Woman:	It's a very bad line. Can you say that again?
Man:	*Can I call you back in a few minutes?*
Woman:	This is Kim speaking.
Man:	Thank you for calling *(breaking up, inaudible . . .)*
Woman:	You're breaking up. I'll call you back.
Man:	Nice to talk to you. 'Bye.

3 👥 This is a telephone role play. It's in two parts so that both students have a chance to make and receive a call. (See **Activities 11** and **31** for full details.) Make sure everyone understands what they have to do before they make their calls. Discourage them from making eye contact during the calls.

At the end
Try another telephone role play, this time a personal one with the two people asking about each other's recent activities – and their plans for the next few days and weeks.

19 Work

19A Earning a living
19B The ideal job?

The aims of **19A** and **19B** are:

- to encourage students to talk about different kinds of jobs
- to revise relative clauses
- to practise the use of near-synonyms
- to practise writing formal letters

Find a job you like and you add five days to every week. – H. Jackson Brown, Jr
Hard work spotlights the character of people: some turn up their sleeves, some turn up their noses, and some don't turn up at all. – Sam Ewing
The only place success comes before work is in the dictionary. – Donald Kendall
One machine can do the work of fifty ordinary men. No machine can do the work of one extraordinary man.
    – Elbert Hubbard

The future

19A Earning a living

A suitable job?

1 👥 At the end, ask the pairs to report on their discussion. What are the jobs they think are exclusively male or female territory?

2 👥 **Suggested answers** – many variations are possible

assembly line worker · factory   builder · building site   caretaker · school   cashier · bank
chambermaid · hotel   chef · restaurant   cleaner · office, school, hospital, etc.
farmer · farm   flight attendant · plane   lecturer · university   lifeguard · beach
machine operator · factory   manager · bank, hotel, restaurant, shop, factory, etc.
musician · recording studio, theatre   nurse · hospital   postman · outdoors
producer · recording studio, theatre, television studio   receptionist · hotel, office
seaman · ship   shop assistant · shop   surgeon · hospital   waiter/waitress · restaurant

3 👥+👥 For example, other people who work outdoors are:

police officers, gardeners, street cleaners, traffic wardens, forestry workers, park keepers, etc.

Relative clauses

Typical mistakes
See **3** in the Student's Book.

1 If possible ask students to look at this page before coming to class.

2 👥 **Answers**

the man who told me about you	= the man spoke to me about you
the man you told me about	= you spoke to me about the man
She is the person that you need to see.	= You need to see that woman.
She is the person who needs to see you.	= That woman needs to see you.
My friend, whose name is Tim, lives nearby.	= I have only one (special) friend and his name is Tim – and he lives near here.
My friend whose name is Tim lives nearby.	= I have many friends and the one called Tim lives near here.

3 👥 **Answers**

1   Her father, who has lived alone since her mother died, will be 80 this year. *(commas needed)*
2   I didn't get the job <u>that</u> I wanted. / I didn't get the job I wanted.
3   The woman ~~to which~~ you spoke <u>to</u> is the manager. *or* <u>to whom</u> you spoke
4   The man who is wearing glasses is her assistant. *(no commas)*
5   My best friend, <u>whose</u> name is Tim, is moving to America, which is a long way from here.

4 👥 This is a bit complicated but it does put the use of relative clauses into a suitable, amusing context. Make sure everyone knows what to do – see **Activities 12** and **32** for details, and point out the speech balloon, which shows students what to say.

Words with similar meanings

1 Deal with any questions arising from this. There are not many words that are exact synonyms – most words with similar meanings are used in different collocations or have slightly different shades of meaning.

2 👥 **Suggested answers**

Similar means nearly the same; *identical* means exactly the same.

A *job* means any kind of work; *a profession* is a job you need special qualifications for, like being a doctor, lawyer, architect, or teacher.

A *warm day* is a day when the temperature is higher than usual; *a hot day* is a day when it's much warmer.

A *big city* is a city with many inhabitants or covering a large area; *a huge city* is a very big city, like New York or Mexico City.

A *cold room* is a room where the temperature is too low; *a cool room* is one which is not warm, but might still be a pleasant temperature.

A *friend* is someone you know well; *an acquaintance* is someone you don't know very well.

A *friend* is someone you socialize with; *a colleague* is someone you work or study with.

A *funny film* makes you laugh; *a hilarious film* makes you laugh a lot.

A *laugh* shows your amusement out loud; *a smile* only shows it on your face.

A *scream* expresses fright or extreme pleasure (usually you can't control a scream); *a shout* expresses anger, or attracts someone's attention (usually you can control a shout).

A *small village* means a place where people live that's much smaller than a town; *a tiny village* is a very small place, with only a few houses.

An *accident* is something that happens without anyone wanting it to, like when someone is run over in the street; *a disaster* involves thousands of people, like an earthquake or when a ship sinks.

An *interview* is when someone talks to you to see if you're suitable for a job, or when a person is asked questions for a newspaper or TV programme; *a conversation* is when people are talking socially, for no special purpose.

A *discussion* is when people talk about a topic; *an argument* develops when they lose their tempers during a discussion and can't agree.

Cross means slightly angry; *furious* means very angry.

Don't be silly means be serious; *don't be stupid* means you are not being intelligent.

We say *don't worry* if someone is likely to be anxious; we say *don't panic* if they are likely to be terrified.

At the end

Ask the class to think of some more words with similar meanings, for example:

little · small   wages · salary   woman · lady · girl

and explain the differences.

19B The ideal job?

My week

1 To save time, students should read this before the lesson.

2 👥 **Answers**

1 New Year's Day 1953 (50 years ago)

2 Because his father was a postman

3 The weather (sometimes), dark winter mornings

Work

4   Lots of breakfasts on the farms
5   To give a talk about the post office
6   The company (of colleagues) and morning chats
7   So that he could say he had worked for exactly 50 years.
8   Civil servant   about the same time that Gareth retires

3   👥 **Answers**

¶3   have a laugh with the boys
¶4   does get me down
      take the rough with the smooth
¶6   company   get on each other's nerves

4   👥 then 👥👥 **After a few minutes, expand the pairs into groups.**

A formal letter

Writing

1   👥 **Suggested arrangement** (Corrections are <u>underlined</u>.)

	742 Evergreen Terrace
	Springfield SP8 4UJ 3
David Brown	
General Manager	
Panorama Hotel	
Springfield SP1 5QY 2	
	29 February 2004 1

<u>Post of part-time receptionist</u>   4
Dear Mr Brown,   5

With reference to your <u>advertisement</u> in the Springfield Shopper, I would like to apply for the post of receptionist.   12

I am 18 years old and a student at Springfield University, where I am studying Business and Marketing. I am in good health and am available to work every evening from 6 pm until late.   7

I could attend an interview at any time <u>convenient</u> to you, but preferably after 5 pm.   8

Looking forward to hearing from you,   11

Yours <u>sincerely</u>,   13

Jo Miller   9

Jo Miller   10

I enclose a photograph and a copy of my CV.   6

2   ✏️ **This could be a fantasy job, or a realistic one!**

20 Transport

20A On the road
20B By land, sea and air

The aims of **20A** and **20B** are:

- to encourage students to talk about different kinds of transport and journeys they have made
- to revise the use of conjunctions to join sentences
- to practise collocations with *look*, *see* and *watch*
- to practise writing paragraphs
- to practise making requests and asking someone for permission

> *If you don't know where you are going, every road will get you nowhere.* – Henry Kissinger
> *To know the road ahead, ask those coming back.* – Chinese proverb
> *Why do they call it rush hour when nothing moves?* – Robin Williams
> *Where there is a sea there are pirates.* – Greek proverb

20A On the road

Traffic in cities

Reading and speaking

1  **Answers**

1 Monday to Friday, 7 am to 6.30 pm
2 £5 per day
3 As many as you like
4 Cameras read your number plate
5 Between 10 pm and midnight you pay £10.
   If you still haven't paid by midnight, you pay £80, reduced to £40 if you pay within 28 days.
   If you still haven't paid after 28 days, the penalty is £120.

2–3 then 👥👥 Expand the pairs into groups later.

Conjunctions

Grammar practice

Typical mistakes

I didn't make the connection while the train was late.
During I was watching TV he phoned me.
I've brought an umbrella if it rains.

1 To save time ask students to read this before the lesson.

2 👥 **Answers** (Conjunctions are <u>underlined</u>.)

<u>After</u> I had bought a magazine, I got on the train.

<u>Even though</u> the train was late I made my connection.

I didn't go by coach <u>because</u> the train was quicker.

The train was late, <u>so</u> I didn't make my connection.

<u>During the time</u> I was on the train I read the magazine.

<u>Before</u> I got on the train I bought a magazine.

The train was late <u>but</u> I made my connection.

I went by train <u>because</u> it was faster than the coach.

I didn't make my connection <u>because</u> the train was late.

I read the magazine <u>while</u> I was on the train.

3 👥 **Answers**

1 even though 2 because/as 3 after
4 before 5 even though 6 while

4 👥 **Suggested answers**

1 I had forgotten to pay the congestion charge so I had to pay £40.
2 I didn't get wet even though it was raining quite hard.
3 We played cards while we were waiting for our plane.
4 We bought some sandwiches before we got on the train.
5 I realized my bag was still on the rack after the train had left.
6 I went by plane even though the ticket was expensive.

Looking, seeing, watching

Vocabulary development

1 👥 This is quite a tricky exercise. If you think your students will find it too difficult, do a couple more examples together as a class first.

Answers

3 If you watch something, you look at it for a long time.
4 If you stare at something, you look for a long time without moving your eyes.
5 If you peek at something, you look quickly and secretly.
6 If you spot something, you see it after looking hard for it.
7 If you notice something, you see it and are aware of it.
8 If you glance at something, you look for a short time.
9 If you observe something, you watch it carefully.

2 👥 **Answers**

1 looking seen 2 look see 3 looking seeing
4 stare see/notice looking/staring 5 watched/saw looks/looked

3 👥 Ask everyone to use full sentences in their answers, to practise using *seeing* verbs.

4 👥 This is a memory game – see **Activity 42** and also **Activity 33** for full details. Make sure everyone understands and follows the instructions.

At the end

If the students enjoyed this game, try another with a poster or with a photo on an overhead transparency.

20B By land, sea and air

How did you travel?

1 👥 The people in the photo are the speakers in **2**.

2 🔊 Pause after each speaker.

Answers

Kim	Rick	Nancy	Andy
By car	By plane	By train	By sea
Because we had a lot of luggage	Because it was too far to drive to Greece	Because it was cheaper than the plane	Parents' 25th wedding anniversary – a treat for his mum
8 hours	6 hours	6 hours (or 30 hours?)	2 weeks
Good music on CD player – they all sang along	Good movie he hadn't seen before	Nothing	Interesting places Spending time with parents Cruising was fun
Forgot to pack camera	Luggage went to another country, they wasted a day getting it back	Trains cancelled because of strike. No seats available on the train next day	Not a thing!

Transcript (Some tricky words are underlined.) 3 minutes 30 seconds

Presenter: Listen to four people talking about journeys they made.

Interviewer: Kim, can you tell us about the last long journey you went on?

Kim: Er…yes. It was last summer, we were going to Cornwall and we went by car because we had a lot of luggage. Um…the whole journey door to door took eight hours.

Interviewer: Eight hours!

Kim: I know it was a…er…a long time, but we stopped for lunch on the way and in the afternoon we stopped again for another break, so . . . The traffic was a <u>nightmare</u>, but the journey went quickly because we had some good music on the CD player and we all <u>sang along</u>. We had a lovely journey, nothing went wrong at all.

Interviewer: Oh, that's not bad going!

Kim: Oh and no, n…no just a minute, w…yeah, one thing did go wrong: I forgot to pack my camera, so I had to buy a <u>disposable</u> one for the holiday. The photos I took with it weren't very good.

Interviewer: Oh, what a shame! Um…how about you, Rick?

Rick: Er…well, last summer we went to…er…we were going to Greece. We went by plane, because you can't…you can't drive all the way to Greece, obviously, it's a bit too far.

Interviewer: Bit far, yes.

Rick: Um…the flight was three hours, but we, you know, you have to get to the airport to check in early, all that. And then there were problems with the luggage at the other end, so that…the whole journey door-to-door took about six hours.

Interviewer: Oh, six hours.

Rick:	Yes, not too bad, you know, I like flying so the flight was OK – they showed a good movie and I hadn't seen that before. Um…but when we arrived nobody's luggage was there!
Interviewer:	Oh, no!
Rick:	You know, they…they…it turned out they'd put it on the wrong plane and it went to Spain or somewhere . . .
Interviewer:	Oh disaster!
Rick:	So we all had to go back to the airport the next day to get it. Y…at least they provided a coach to take us there so, you know, that wasn't too bad. But, oh, it was a wasted day.
Interviewer:	Oh, it sounds very tiresome. Er…Nancy?
Nancy:	That's nothing! We were going to go by plane, but the train was cheaper so we went by train – and it was an absolute nightmare!
Interviewer:	No, why?
Nancy:	W…we'd booked our seats and arrived at the station on time. Then we discovered there was a <u>strike</u> and all trains were <u>cancelled</u>.
Interviewer:	Oh dear!
Nancy:	We went home and returned the next morning. And, of course, there weren't enough seats for everybody and we had to sit on our suitcases all the way, and the whole journey took six hours, or one day and six hours if you count the day we missed.
Interviewer:	Oh dear, I'm sorry to hear that.
Nancy:	It was awful.
Interviewer:	Um…what about you? Andy?
Andy:	Well, we went by sea. It was a…it was a Mediterranean <u>cruise</u> and…um…well, we went with my parents because it was their 25th <u>wedding anniversary</u> and my mum had never been on a cruise, she always wanted to, so we…um…we <u>treated</u> her. Um…the whole cruise lasted two weeks, um…starting from Venice in Italy and going all the way down the Italian coast and then around the Greek islands, and we called at some really interesting places. It was…it was great.
Interviewer:	Lovely.
Andy:	It was great to spend time with my parents, um…that…that was really the best thing about it, but e…even cruising was great, better…better than I'd thought it was going to be. Really, really enjoyable.
Interviewer:	And did anything go wrong?
Andy:	Um…well, um…no, not a thing!
Interviewer:	Brilliant!

3 👥 **Answer**

Nancy probably had the worst journey.

Paragraphs

Writing

1 👥 The answer is, of course, because it is divided into paragraphs. The second section looks like a mess, and it's harder to read.

Paragraphs show the readers where each new idea is, giving them a chance to stop reading for a moment and then easily find their place again. Leaving a line between paragraphs also breaks up a text and makes it easier to find your way around.

And, in an exam, leaving a line empty means you can return to that paragraph and make some changes in the available space, if necessary.

Main themes of 'Traffic'

¶1   Traffic levels   ¶2   Traffic flow *or* Traffic flowed well   ¶3   Bus services

'Operations', with paragraphs:

Almost half a million payments are expected to have been made this week by midnight on Friday 28 February. Payments of the charge for each day throughout the week were:

- 93,000 (Monday)
- 97,000 (Tuesday)
- 99,000 (Wednesday)
- 98,000 (Thursday)
- Payments for today (Friday) are still being made.

In total, around 30,000 Penalty Charge Notices are expected to be issued for the week. Payment channels (text messaging, retail, web and call centre) generally worked well throughout the week although there was an interruption to the web payment facility for a short period late on Thursday evening.

A TfL spokesperson said:
'The smooth start to the scheme is continuing with traffic levels still well down on a normal working week. The system is working well dealing with many thousands of successful transactions every day.'

2   ✎   **Maybe set a word limit for this? About 150 words?**

Remember to allow time for students to read each other's work, and suggest improvements, before they hand it in to you for correction.

Model version

I love going by bike. The feeling of freedom you get from sailing along under your own power, not having to wait for a bus to arrive, not having to find somewhere to park, not having to worry about timetables – all this makes riding a bike a joyful experience.

Of course, in bad weather, cycling is not quite so much fun. In rain you get wet not only from above but also from being splashed by passing traffic. But if you have waterproof clothes, that doesn't matter so much. You can freeze in cold weather, but if you wear warm clothes and gloves you can still feel comfortable.

But in hot weather there's no better way to travel. You create your own air-conditioning as you pedal along. And away from busy roads, you can breathe in the fresh air and go as fast – or as slowly – as you like. Imagine a lovely sunny day, not a cloud in the sky, as you fly down a long hill, the wind in your hair. Marvellous!

There's really only one big disadvantage of cycling: going up hills!

© Cambridge University Press, 2005

Transport

Requesting and asking permission

1 🔊 👥 No doubt which people were more polite!

Transcript (Phrases used are in **bold**.) 30 seconds

Presenter: Listen to two conversations.

Woman: I need a pen.
Man: Do you?
Woman: Lend me yours.
Man: Here you are.
Woman: Got any paper?
Man: No.

Woman: **Er… could you lend me** a pencil?
Man: **Of course, here you are.**
Woman: Thanks very much.
Man: **Oh, may I borrow your** newspaper?
Woman: **Sure.**
Man: Thanks.
Woman: Don't mention it.

2 🔊 👥 The sentences are recorded with pauses for repetition.

Transcript (1 minute 20 seconds)

Presenter: Practise saying these phrases.

Man: I say, could you lend me a pen, please ?
Woman: Er…could you lend me a pencil ?
Man: Please will you lend me some paper?
Woman: Can you lend me a rubber?
Man: Oh, may I borrow your book?
Woman: Can I borrow your dictionary?
Man: Is it all right if I borrow your ruler?

Woman: Sure.
Man: Certainly.
Woman: Of course, here you are.
Man: I'm afraid not, because I need it.
Woman: No, sorry. You see I need it myself.
Man: Well, the problem is I can't.

3 👤 then 👥 If students need some inspiration, make a list of some things on the board to start them off:

lend me	a dictionary	your bicycle	some money
give me	some paper	a pen some help	some advice
open	the window	the door	
borrow	your dictionary	your rubber your ruler	your notes

16–20 Revision

Topic vocabulary

Answers

16 Words from Unit 16

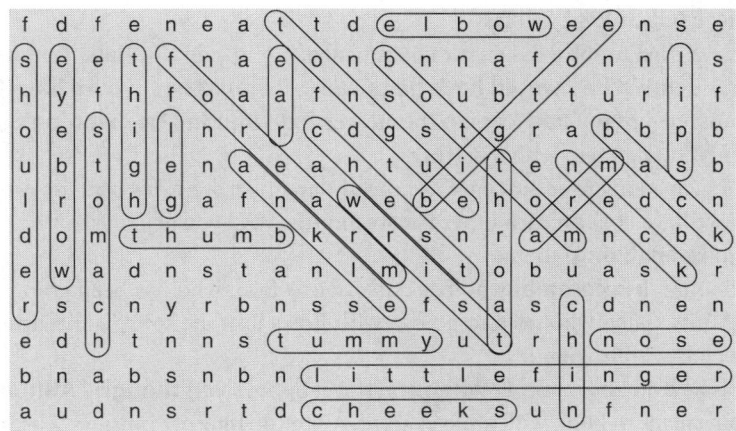

18 Words from Unit 18

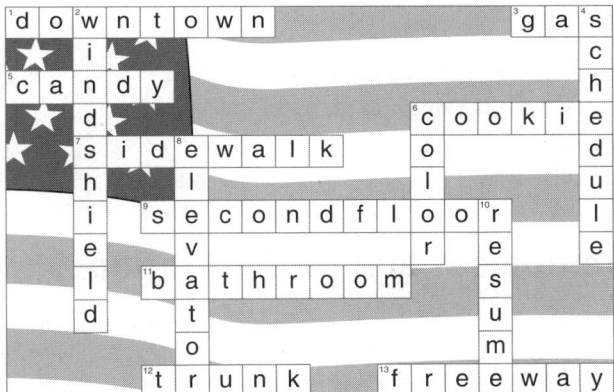

19 Words from Unit 19

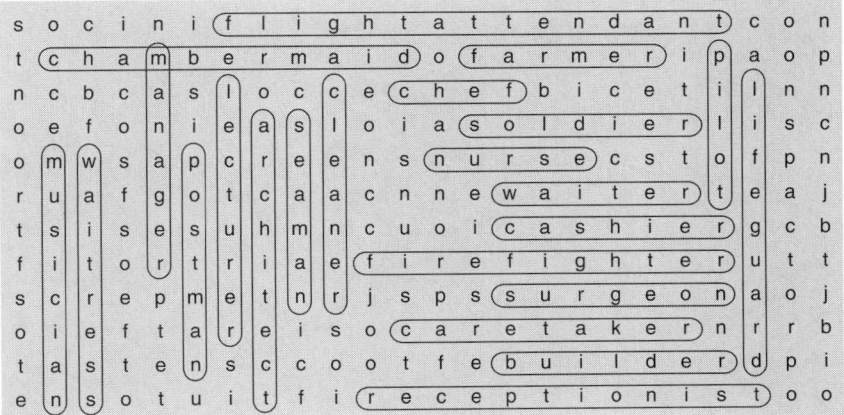

Grammar review

A Answers (Ø = no article)

16 Bob wanted to join **a** health club, but **the** membership subscription for **the** private one near to **his** flat was too expensive, so he went to **a/the** public leisure centre in **the** town centre, opposite **the** station. He enrolled on **a** course with **a** fitness instructor, but after **a** couple of sessions he decided that **the** classes were **a** waste of time. Then he took **some/Ø** swimming lessons, which were **a** great success. Now he goes to **the** pool every day in **the** morning before he has **his** breakfast.

17 I have tried to solve the puzzles on my own, but in vain. If I **had / had had** someone to help me, it **would be / would have been** easier. It **would be / would have been** easier still if someone **knew / had known** the answer, but **wouldn't be / wouldn't have been** so much fun as doing them with a partner.

18 It's such a long time **since** we last met. I remember we **were** both in London six months **ago**, so we haven't **seen** each other **for** six months. And you're living in Paris now. How long **have** you **been (living)** there?

19 The man **(no comma)** who has curly hair is Bob**,** who has been going out with Sally for six months. Sally**,** who used to go out with Bob's brother Tony**,** is the sister of Mary**,** who used to be Bob's girlfriend!

20 You have to book a ticket **when** you travel by air. **Even though / Although** it may be more convenient to book with a travel agent, using the Internet is usually cheaper. Booking early is also a good idea **as/because** it's cheaper than waiting **until** there are only a few days left **before** you go.

B Suggested answers

16 healthy food   stay in
17 would have felt less frustrated if he had been
18 has been living / has lived in this country for
19 even though the traffic was
20 who is a basketball player,

Vocabulary development and pronunciation

Answers

16 accidéntally   operátion   photógraphy   módern   Ápril   Fébruary
17 make   take   take   make   do
18 lift   trousers   holiday   post code   motorway
19 disappear   sad/miserable   approximately   exactly   cross/annoyed
20 forward to   for
      after   at

21 The past

21A Do you remember?
21B A very long time ago

The aims of **21A** and **21B** are:

- to encourage students to talk about their memories, milestones in their lives, and about history

- to revise modal verbs in the past

- to practise recognizing how tones of voice show a speaker's mood

- to practise checking spelling when proof-reading your own work

- to practise speaking and writing about your own experiences

> *A generation which ignores history has no past and no future.* – Robert Heinlein
> *After hearing two eyewitness accounts of the same accident, you begin to wonder about history.*
> *This is the greatest week in the history of the world since the Creation.* – Richard M. Nixon saluting the crew of Apollo 11
> *Nothing is more responsible for the good old days than a bad memory.* – Robert Benchley
> *The advantage of a bad memory is that one enjoys several times the same good things for the first time.* – Friedrich Nietzsche
> *A good storyteller is a person who has a good memory and hopes other people haven't.* – Irvin Shrewsbury Cobb
> *Each happiness of yesterday is a memory for tomorrow.* – George W. Douglas
> *I would not say that the future is necessarily less predictable than the past. I think the past was…was not predictable when it started.* – Donald Rumsfeld, US Secretary of Defense

21A Do you remember?

Memories and history

Speaking and vocabulary

1–2 then  The first two activities encourage students to talk about their own pasts. The questions are suitable for students who are in their teens. Older students won't have time to reach last year in **2**, but they could remember *some* recent years, as well as their childhood.

3   **Answers**

1 prehistoric   monument   BC   Archaeologists
2 ancient   destroyed   restored
3 Revolution   republic   Emperor   invaded   retreat
4 century   empires   War   colonies   independence   states

Modal verbs – 2

Typical mistakes

I musted to pay a lot of money.
You shouldn't paid so much.
I didn't can find my wallet.
He mustn't have remembered our date.

1 Ask students to do this before they come to class.

2 👥 **Answers**

B You must have paid a lot of money.   = The price was probably very high.
You had to pay a lot of money.   = The price was very high.
You shouldn't have paid a lot of money.   = You paid too much.

C She can't have done it by herself.   = I'm fairly sure she had some help.
She couldn't do it by herself.   = She wasn't able to do it without help.
She shouldn't have done it by herself.   = She needed help, but she didn't ask for it.
She should have done it by herself.   = She was wrong to ask for help.

D He might have lost your phone number.   = It's possible he has lost it.
He must have lost your number.   = He has probably lost it.
He can't have lost your number.   = It's impossible that he has lost it.

3 👥 **Answers**

1 would have / 'd have / could have   **2** must have   **3** shouldn't have
4 must have / might have   must have / might have
5 could / was able to   had to   **6** can't / couldn't have been   must / could have been

4 👥 Students use the phrases in Activities 13 and 34 to guess why the two people were late for work.

Recognizing tones of voice

1 🔊👥 **Transcript and Answers** 1 minute 30 seconds

Presenter: Listen to six speakers and decide what their moods are. First Alice.

Alice (*sincere*): Thank you for telling us that lovely story about your childhood. It was really interesting and I think we all enjoyed it . . .

Presenter: Now Ben.
Ben (*sarcastic*): Well, thank you for telling us that *lovely* story about your childhood. It was *really* interesting and I think we all enjoyed . . .

Presenter: Now Carl.
Carl (*angry*): We had to wait so long that we not only missed the beginning of the film but we could only get seats at the side of the cinema so we had a terrible view . . .

Presenter: Now Donna.
Donna (*disappointed*): We had to wait so long that we not only missed the beginning of the film, but we could only get seats at the side of the cinema so we had a terrible view . . .

Presenter: Now Ellie.
Ellie (*nervous*): Ooh, I have to give a talk to the class tomorrow about my hobby. I've made all these notes so, oh, I hope it goes well and that everybody actually listens to me . . .

Presenter: Now Frank.

Frank (*confident*): I have to give a talk to the class tomorrow about my hobby. I've made all these notes, so I hope it goes well and that everyone listens . . .

2 👥 If everyone is finding this fun, ask some pairs to perform in front of the whole class, but with their backs turned. Can the others recognize the mood from the tone of voice (without seeing the speakers' faces)?

21B A very long time ago

The thrill of history

Reading

1 👥 This remarkable photo, an early example of *real* colour photography, is one of a series of scenes of the Russian Empire, taken by Sergei Mikhailovich Prokudin-Gorskii in the early years of the 20th century. More can be seen at the US Library of Congress website: www.loc.gov/exhibits/empire, together with background information about each photograph.

2 👥 **Suggested answers**

1 Five (or more, if we include: we have nothing in common, they are distant, strange and unreal): they wore funny clothes, they spoke languages nobody speaks any more, they had strange religions, they had no modern equipment or gadgets, they didn't watch television like we do

2 Because he can identify with them, using hard evidence and his imagination.

3 They are not the way to experience the thrill of history.

4 Because imagining the way people lived in the past is thrilling.

5 The ruins of their cities, their art which shows them looking like modern people, their preserved bodies

3 👥 **Answers**

¶1 have in common
¶2 reincarnation   reach back   hard evidence   chariots
¶3 make the leap   addiction
¶4 on a gut level   eerily   exquisitely preserved

Check your spelling

Writing

1 👥 **Answers**

2	ago	**3**	lives	**4**	similar	**5**	stories
6	traditional	**7**	happenings	**8**	of	**9**	tales
10	happened	**11**	differently	**12**	truth		

2 👥 This should be done in pairs with students helping each other to decide which mistakes they should or could have spotted.

At the end
Find out from the class if there are any mistakes that lots of them make. This may reassure students that others have similar difficulties.

Your experiences

1   👤 Making notes will help students to remember details and later to remember what they remembered.

2   👥 Encourage students to ask each other questions to find out more about each event.

3   ✎ Remind everyone that their stories are going to be read by other students in **4**. Partly true stories are most fun, then the others will have to guess which parts are true and untrue.

4   👥👥 Groups of four or five for this.

At the end
Point out that in the FCE exam, if they choose to write a story, it needn't be true – how could the examiners tell if it was, anyway?

22 The news

22A Keep up to date
22B What's in the news?

The aims of **22A** and **22B** are:

* to encourage students to talk about news events, current affairs and the media
* to revise the use of prepositions
* to practise the spelling and pronunciation of homonyms and homophones
* to practise writing a short report

> *For most folks, no news is good news; for the press, good news is not news.* – Gloria Borger
> *It's amazing that the amount of news that happens in the world every day just exactly fits in the newspaper.*
>   – Jerry Seinfeld
> *Newspapers are unable, seemingly, to discriminate between a bicycle accident and the collapse of civilization.*
>   – George Bernard Shaw
> *Those who cast the votes decide nothing. Those who count the votes decide everything.* – Joseph Stalin

22A Keep up to date

What happened?

1   👥 The first picture shows police officers in Germany protesting about the abolition of the mounted police division. The second shows spectators in a hot tub watching the Iditarod Trail Sled Dog Race in Fairbanks, Alaska.

2   👥 First, ask everyone to look at the headlines. Are there words (e.g. *serial killer*) that they don't understand? And are there any adjectives in the list that need to be explained?

3 ⬤⬤⬤⬤ At the end, ask each group to give a brief report on their findings.

Prepositions – 2

Typical mistakes

Congratulations for your succes.
She hit him by a piece of wood.
I was listening my Walkman.
Please get away the door.

1 Try to get them to read this section before the lesson if possible.

2 👥 **Answers**

Everyone praised him	*for*	his performance in the concert.
I find it hard to concentrate	*on*	my homework with the TV on.
That story reminds me	*of*	a funny thing that happened to me.
We congratulated him	*on*	doing so well in the exam.
I can't forgive him	*for*	telling lies and cheating in the exam.
He tried to blame us	*for*	his own stupidity.
They named their son	*after*	David Beckham.
I spent all evening preparing	*for*	the next day's test.
He punished his son	*for*	speaking to me so rudely.

3 👥 **Answers**

A woman came home **from** work and found her husband **in** the kitchen. She was terrified because he was shaking all over **with** what looked like a wire running **to/from** his waist **from/to** the electric kettle. She wanted to get him away **from** the deadly current, so she hit him **with** a large piece **of** wood that was lying **near/outside/inside/by** the back door, and broke his arm **in** two places. This was a pity because the man had only been listening **to** his Walkman.

Spelling and pronunciation

1 🔊 👥 These words are homonyms. First the students should take turns to read the sentences aloud. Then they hear the model versions (1 minute 10 seconds).

2 👥 And these are homophones. Encourage students to follow the pattern in the speech balloons as they look at the list. They should use a dictionary for this task.

22B What's in the news?

Here is the news . . .

1 🔊 The students hear the recording twice. First they just have to get the main points.

Answers

'Help, we are being kidnapped!'	Austria
Homeless – thanks to the cat	Germany

Moldovans snorkel to new life   Calgary, Canada
Teacher nearly killed by books   Zagreb, Croatia
'Twice is enough'   Amsterdam, Holland

2 **During the second listening they have to listen out for specific information.**

Answers

1 visas   sports   1,200
2 neighbour   noises   60   maths   move
3 sisters   aunt   sign   arrested   released   pleased/happy
4 3   foreigners   mouth   (over) 200   twice
5 bath   ceiling   stairs   dinner   fire   destroyed   repaired/fixed

Transcript   3 minutes 30 seconds

Presenter: Listen to a radio news programme.

(*music*)

Nigel: Welcome to *News From Around The World* with me, Nigel Green . . .

Amy: . . . and me, Amy Brown.

Nigel: And our first story comes from Canada, where the World Underwater Hockey Championships are being held this month. One team didn't turn up for the championships in Calgary – the women's team from Moldova. Because they were members of an international sports team, the women were able to get visas to enter Canada. They each paid $1,200 to a people-smuggler who made all the arrangements with the Moldovan Underwater Hockey Federation. Since entering Canada none of the women have been seen.

Amy: A teacher in Zagreb, Croatia, had a lucky escape thanks to his neighbour who heard strange noises coming from his flat. His wife was in hospital and she phoned the neighbour because he hadn't visited her for so long. The neighbour called the police and they broke down the door and found the 60-year-old maths teacher under a pile of books in his bed. The bookshelf above the bed had fallen down and the man was unable to move from under the books. He is now recovering in hospital.

Nigel: It could happen to anyone! Two young sisters were travelling on the motorway in a car with their aunt in Lower Austria yesterday. They put a sign in the car window saying 'Help! We're being kidnapped.' Another motorist saw the sign and called the police on his mobile. The police stopped the aunt and arrested her. Later the sisters admitted it was just a joke and the aunt was released. We don't know what she said to her nieces, but she was certainly not pleased.

Amy: A former university lecturer in Amsterdam, Holland, has started a campaign against Dutch people giving each other three kisses when they meet. He said, 'Giving three kisses is a habit taken from the south of the country, but it is useless and without any meaning. Nowhere in Europe, except in Belgium, do people give each other three kisses to say hello. Foreigners are quite upset when they have to give three kisses – especially when the third kiss is on the mouth! All books about good manners prescribe only one, and on some occasions two, kisses.' He has distributed over 200 badges saying: 'Twice is enough'. He says by wearing the badges, people are showing they only want to be kissed twice.

Nigel: Haha! Well, I know where I'm moving! And now a bad luck story from Germany about a couple who are homeless, thanks to their cat. Elsie and Walter Kochentopf's cat, Robbie, was playing with the bath tap and accidentally turned it on. The couple were in the front room watching television when they saw water dripping from the ceiling. The water was flowing down the stairs and into the cellar. They started removing all their possessions from the cellar to save them from the flood. But they forgot about their dinner which was cooking in the kitchen. This started a fire that destroyed the kitchen and the hallway. The couple, and their cat, are now homeless while their house is being repaired.

Amy: And finally, the weather for this weekend, over to Michael Brown at the Weather Centre. Michael.

Michael: Yes, hello. Well, it's going to be a nice day . . . on Tuesday. Until then, I'm afraid, it's going to be cold and . . .

Writing a report

1 👥 Plenty of good advice here! Filling the gaps encourages the students to discover the advice and may help them to remember it better.

Answers
¶1 event   readers
¶2 points   order   details   direct speech   life
¶3 scene   interest   informed   impressed

2 🔊 Students will need to hear this news broadcast at least twice. Pause the recording where necessary.

Transcript 2 minutes 20 seconds

Presenter: Listen to this news story and make notes on the main points.

Woman: They wanted to win a million pounds on the TV quiz show *Who Wants To Be A Millionaire?*, but they could only do it by cheating.

Man: Major Charles Ingram, his wife Diana and lecturer Tecwen Whittock were found guilty of cheating to win a million pounds on *Who Wants To Be A Millionaire?* Diana and her brother had both been on the show before and won £32,000 each. But she wanted her husband to win the biggest prize, so they worked out a plan to beat the system. They met a college lecturer, Tecwen Whittock, and he agreed to help them.

Woman: On the night Chris Tarrant, the host, had Charles Ingram opposite him in the 'hot seat' and was going for the top prize, and Tecwen Whittock was sitting a few feet behind him, among the other contestants waiting for a chance to play.

Man: The questions in the show are multiple-choice, but Charles Ingram didn't know the answers to most of the questions, so his trick was to say each of the four alternative answers out loud. Then Tecwen Whittock, who did know the answers, would cough when he said the correct answer, and Charles Ingram would know which answer to give. Everyone in the audience was amazed at the way Ingram kept guessing correct answers, often after rejecting them.

Woman: Altogether 19 coughs were heard in the studio when Major Ingram said the correct answer out loud; except once, when the cough was followed by a man's voice saying 'No'.

Man: Celador, the company which makes *Who Wants To Be A Millionaire?*, suspected they had been cheated and refused to pay the £1 million cheque to Major Ingram. He tried to sue them to get the money but 18 months later he was in court – on trial for fraud. The jury in the case found the three guilty. The Ingrams were fined £15,000 each and given 18-month suspended prison sentences. Whittock, the man who coughed, was fined £10,000 and given a 12-month suspended prison sentence.

Woman: Now Celador are planning to make a movie of the whole story!

3 ✎ Set a word limit for this: about 150 words should be about right. (In the FCE exam the word-limit is 120–180 words.)

I read in the paper . . .

1 👥 The students should read the stories in **Activities 15** and **35** carefully before they start telling each other. Highlighting the main points will help them to remember the story without having to quote verbatim.

2 ✎ About 150 words again.

23 Books

23A Reading for pleasure
23B A good read

The aims of **23A** and **23B** are:

- to encourage students to talk about books they have enjoyed, recommend books to each other, and to read 'readers' in English
- to revise the use of gerunds and infinitives
- to practise using common compound words
- to practise spotting mistakes in written work

A home without books is a body without soul. – Marcus Tullius Cicero
A book is like a garden carried in the pocket. – Chinese proverb
I'm trying to read a book on how to relax, but I keep falling asleep. – Jim Loy
The pleasure of all reading is doubled when one lives with another who shares the same books.
  – Katherine Mansfield
You know you've read a good book when you turn the last page and feel a little as if you have lost a friend. –
  Paul Sweeney
Reading is the basics [basis] for all learning. – George W. Bush

23A Reading for pleasure

What do you read?

1 👥 Sadly, many young people read few books. But they do read magazines – and they read information on websites. This counts as reading too.
Ask the students, 'What's missing from the list that you read often?'

2 👥 The list in this activity contains a lot of useful vocabulary for this topic.

3 👥 And there is more useful vocabulary in this exercise.

Answers

10 Best Sherlock Holmes Stories	Crime
100 Wonderful English Recipes	Cookery
1000 Great Inventions	Science and technology
A Complete Atlas of the World	Reference
Basketball Skills and Drills	Sports
Eyewitness Guide to the Greek Islands	Travel
Great Expectations by Charles Dickens	Literature
Harry Potter . . . read by Stephen Fry	Audio books
Help Yourself to a Better Memory	Self-help
The Friendly Dragon	Children's
The Invisible Man	Science fiction
The Life of Charles Dickens	Biography
The New Book of Vitamins	Health
The Second World War	History

–ing and *to . . .* – 2

Grammar practice

Typical mistakes

I can't sneeze without to close my eyes.
I couldn't help to sneeze.
Would you like joining me for dinner?

1 To save time, ask students to read this before the lesson.

2 👥 **Suggested answers**

2 making any mistakes at all
3 closing your eyes
4 holding your breath for a long time
5 bending your knees
6 blinking once
7 dozing off for even a minute

3 👥 **Answers**

1	I can't afford	to go out every night.
2	I gave up	trying to phone him after getting no answer.
3	I couldn't help	laughing when I saw her new hairstyle.
4	Will you please help me	to translate this report?
5	She keeps on	complaining about everything.
6	I'd like you	to make the phone call for me.
7	I don't mind	waiting for you if you're not quite ready.
8	He persuaded me	to go with him to the concert.
9	Would you prefer	to see a film rather than go out for a meal?
10	I pretended	not to notice when he shouted at me.

Two-word words

1 👥 There are no 'rules' for whether compound words are one word or two words. Students just have to notice and try to remember. (If in doubt use two words.)

Answers

air conditioning	airline	airmail	airport	
bookmark	bookshelf	book club	bookshop	bookworm
headache	headlight	head office	headphones	
newspaper	newsletter	news conference		
paperback	paper clip	paper weight		
police officer	policeman	police station		

birthday card	credit card	postcard	
boyfriend	girlfriend	best friend	
bus stop	full stop		
homework	housework		
library book	notebook	phone book	
mailing list	reading list	shopping list	waiting list

2 👥 **Answers**

24-hour	absent-minded	all-day	all-night	brand-new
first-class	home-made	kind-hearted	left-handed	long-lost/-sighted
old-fashioned	one-handed	self-service	short-sighted	well-known

At the end
See if anyone can think of more examples, using the words in **2**, for example:
half-hearted   right-handed   self-satisfied   well-read

23B A good read

Chapter 1

1 🔊👥 The extracts, which are recorded, come from two of the excellent Cambridge Readers series, and from the first of Lemony Snicket's *Series of Unfortunate Events* books – an easier, shorter and more entertaining read than *Harry Potter* – which your students might enjoy reading in English.

(The three readings last 6 minutes altogether.)

This is the blurb from the back cover of *The Bad Beginning*:

Dear Reader,

I'm sorry to say that the book you are holding in your hands is extremely unpleasant. It tells an unhappy tale about three very unlucky children. Even though they are charming and clever, the Baudelaire siblings lead lives filled with misery and woe. From the very first page of this book when the children are at the beach and receive terrible news, continuing on through the entire story, disaster lurks at their heels. One might say they are magnets for misfortune.

In this short book alone, the three youngsters encounter a greedy and repulsive villain, itchy clothing, a disastrous fire, a plot to steal their fortune, and cold porridge for breakfast.

It is my sad duty to write down these unpleasant tales, but there is nothing stopping you from putting this book down at once and reading something happy, if you prefer that sort of thing.

With all due respect,

Lemony Snicket

Sporting mistakes – 2

👥 When the students have finished searching for the mistakes in the two reviews, ask them to look at Activity 37 on page 141, where they'll find model versions with all the corrected mistakes underlined. (If you want to be more picky, there are more mistakes than the ones corrected there.)

The two reviews in Activity 37 are what might be called 'achievable models' – the kind of reviews which students at this level might write themselves when they do the writing task in the next section.

(Did the students spot the deliberate mistake in the title?)

A really good book!

1 👥👥👥 Encourage students to ask each other questions to find out more about each book. (The books can be fiction or non-fiction, low-brow or high-brow.)

2–3 ✎ then 👥 Or even a CD?

Books

24 People

24A Friends
24B Men and women, boys and girls

The aims of **24A** and **24B** are:

- to encourage students to talk about friends and friendship
- to practise some common phrasal verbs
- to practise describing people in speech and in writing

A friend is somebody you want to be around when you feel like being by yourself. – Barbara Burrow
My best friend is the one who brings out the best in me. – Henry Ford
Before borrowing money from a friend it's best to decide which you need most. – Joe Moore
The real test of friendship is: can you literally do nothing with the other person? Can you enjoy those moments of life that are utterly simple? – Eugene Kennedy
When I eventually met Mr Right I had no idea that his first name was Always. – Rita Rudner
What a strange thing man is; and what a stranger thing woman. – Lord Byron
The good people sleep much better at night than the bad people. Of course, the bad people enjoy the waking hours much more. – Woody Allen

24A Friends

Good friends
Speaking and vocabulary

1 👥 then 👥+👥 At the end, ask the groups to share their best stories.

2 👥 then 👥👥👥 Combine the pairs into groups at the end.

3 👥👥👥 Ask the groups to share their answers to the last question with the class.

Two-word verbs
Grammar practice and vocabulary development

Two-word verbs cause students a lot of consternation and confusion. One difficulty is word order, another is the meaning of idiomatic two-word verbs – and even teachers disagree about whether a particular two-word verb is a phrasal verb (verb + adverb particle) or a verb + preposition*. And linguists don't agree on what is a phrasal verb either, which is why this section's title is **Two-word verbs**.

*Some examples, which may help (but probably won't):

bring back in *Bring back my book* is a verb + adverb
run past in *He ran past my house* is a verb + preposition
run past and *look on* in *He ran past while we looked on* are verbs + adverb
look after in *Please look after my cat* is an idiomatic verb + preposition

Typical mistakes
Someone has my glass away taken.
The plane took on time off.
Please hold for a moment on.

1 The best advice for students at this level is probably 'Don't worry!' – and study the examples in the Grammar reference section on pages 129 and 130.

2 **Some suggested answers**

The dog was so frightening that we <u>ran away</u> (from it).

I've finished with these books, so you can <u>take them away</u> now.

I'm leaving now and I'm never <u>coming back</u>!

My suitcase is so heavy I can't <u>lift it up</u>.

When you've finished with those books, please <u>put them back</u> on the shelf.

3 👥 **The sentences which are wrong are:**

c Someone has it away taken. ✗

e Someone has taken away it. ✗

2 He jumped the cliff off. ✗   **5** I was looking them for. ✗

3 She opened up it. ✗   **6** Flowers come in the spring out. ✗

4 **Suggested answers**

2	finished	leave	**3**	cancelled		**4**	published/released
5	out of bed		**6**	not be at home	at home	**7**	return
8	the matter	over/finished					

5 **Answers**

2	take off	go in	**3**	sit back	keep on
4	hold on	come across	**5**	give up	take up
6	get on with	gone off	**7**	turn down	turn it off
8	check in	fill in / fill out			

24B Men and women, boys and girls

Who's who?

Listening

1 👥 Students should use dictionaries if necessary. Clearly, the adjectives they choose are a matter of opinion and guesswork.

2 🔊 Pause after each description for students to write their answers.

If you think the names might be hard to understand, write the names on the board in the same order as they are described in the recording:

Jane   William   Rita   James   Alice   Alex   Graham   Yoko

Be prepared to play the recording twice as students may find it quite difficult.

Transcript and Answers 3 minutes 40 seconds

Presenter: Listen to descriptions of the eight people in the photos.

Woman: Jane is quite **quiet** and quite **reserved** really. She finds it hard to make new friends and I think that's partly because she's so **sensitive**, she gets really disappointed as well. It's silly really because you have to make such an effort to get to know her, you know. And when you do she's a really good friend, she's **reliable** and she's got this really great **imagination** too. – **picture 5**

Man: William, oh William's a great character. He **never stops talking** and…um…he's really quite a **lively** kind of person. Oh, and he's very **kind** to people who need his help, definitely. He's really sweet t…to everyone, actually. Oh, he's also a great cook, so if he ever invites you for a meal, just say 'Yes!' immediately. You'll really enjoy the food and the conversation. – **picture 4**

People

137

Woman: Everyone likes Rita, she's brilliant. She's so **easy-going** and **friendly**. I think that's partly because she's so **considerate**, she's genuinely interested in other people, that's why she makes friends so easily. When you meet her she'll ask you about yourself. You know, she'll make you feel important. She always **dresses really nicely** too. – **picture 6**

Man: James is really **funny**, all the time. He loves playing tricks on people and just generally having a really good laugh. Um…he's actually a really **talented artist** as well, but he's quite **modest** about that, you…you'll never really hear him talking about it. Um…but I think his paintings are really lovely, I really do think, you know, I believe in him, I…I think he could be well known one day, but on the whole he doesn't really take himself seriously enough. – **picture 3**

Woman: Alice is a lovely person, she's always so **cheerful** and she is incredibly **calm**. Nothing ever seems to get to her or worry or upset her. If you've got a problem or you need advice, she's the person to go to. She has these brilliant stories about all the things she's experienced and all the different parts of the world she's been to. – **picture 8**

Man: Alex **looks rather conventional**, that's because he has to wear a suit for work and I suppose, well, yeah, he is quite a **sensible** person, I mean, he works hard and, you know, works long hours – all of that. But…um…away from work he's a totally different person. He really…really lets his hair down, I mean, he can go wild sometimes. No, he…he certainly isn't serious in his private life! – **picture 2**

Man: Graham is quite a serious guy. He actually **looks a little bit arrogant** a…and when you first meet him he does come across as a bit **unfriendly**. But, you know, once you get to know him he's really nice and I think he has a lovely, dry sense of humour. – **picture 1**

Woman: Yoko **looks really shy and timid**. But far from it, underneath she's the most **adventurous** and **sociable** person I know. She speaks five languages fluently and she's **full of confidence**. She'll go up to total strangers and start conversations with them, she'll even make them laugh within seconds. She's really **clever** too. She's brilliant, actually. – **picture 7**

3 👥 This time students should talk about each person's appearance, as well as their personality.

Describing people

Speaking and writing

1 👥 then 👥+👥 **Suggested answers**

Age	elderly	young	in his/her teens
Height	average height	tallish	short
Build	overweight	fat	thin
Hair colour	grey	white	brown
Hairstyle	long	short	curly
Eyes	blue	grey	green
Appearance	pretty	attractive	plain
Clothes	elegant	well-dressed	
	sweatshirt	collar and tie	

2 👥 Unfortunately we don't have any photos of the people from the waist down, so there are no 'correct answers'.

3 👤 then 👥

4 👥 More people to describe in Activities 16 and 36. (These show the same people left to right, and right to left, but don't tell the students this!)

5 ✏️ Word limit about 150 words? Or maybe just 100?

25 That's funny!

25A A sense of humour
25B Ha, ha, ha!

The aims of **25A** and **25B** are:

- to encourage students to enjoy jokes and anecdotes in English, and to talk about humour
- to revise adverbs and word order
- to practise editing written work (to make it shorter)
- to practise telling funny stories

Laughter is the best medicine. – English proverb
Nobody ever died of laughter. – Max Beerbohm

25A A sense of humour

I don't get it!

Speaking and vocabulary

1 👥 Ask the pairs to report back to the class, or expand the pairs into groups.

2 👥 If you have a multicultural class, arrange pairs or groups with mixed cultures. If you have a co-educational class, arrange pairs or groups with mixed genders. Maybe females and males find different things funny?

3 👥 See Activities **18** and **38** to find out how this works.

Adverbs and word order

Grammar practice

Typical mistakes
See the sentences in **2** in the Student's book.

1 Ask students to do this before they come to class.

2 👥 Funny, strange, that is (not funny, ha, ha).

Answers
1 I **never** laugh at practical jokes.
2 Whenever I tell a joke I **always** forget the punch line.
3 When an adverb is put in the wrong place it **often** looks funny.
4 He slipped and **unexpectedly** fell over. *or* fell over **unexpectedly**.
5 **Yesterday** I saw a very funny film.
   or I saw a very funny film **yesterday**.
6 She **hardly ever** gets the jokes I tell.
7 I like funny films **very much**. *or* I **very much** like funny films.
8 I'm going to the cinema **tonight** with my friends.
   or **Tonight** I'm going . . . *or* . . . with my friends **tonight**.
9 Everyone laughed **loudly** when he fell into the swimming pool.
10 **Funnily** enough, I've already seen that film.

3 👥 **Answers**

1 I'm **probably** going to Greece this summer.
2 He's leaving the country **soon**.
3 She plays the piano **very well**.
4 We all laughed **heartily** when he spilt his coffee.
5 I could **hardly** understand what he was saying.
6 **Luckily**, I had my mobile phone with me. *or* I had my mobile phone with me **luckily**.
7 Have you **ever** ridden a motorbike?
8 He **obviously** didn't get the joke.
   or **Obviously** he didn't . . . *or* he didn't get . . . **obviously**.
9 As the door **slowly** opened I **quickly** put away the chocolates.
   or As the door opened **slowly** I put away the chocolates **quickly**.
10 He told me **yesterday** he was going to phone me **today**. *or* **Yesterday** he told me . . .

Reading aloud

Pronunciation

Reading aloud? How can this be justified in the 21st century? Well, from time to time we do have to quote lines or sentences from a book, newspaper or website. This exercise is just a fun way of practising this!

1 🔊 👥 **Read first, then listen.** (40 seconds)

2 👥 + 👥 **More jokes in Activities 19 and 41.**

If there's time here are a few more jokes to share:

How many Californians does it take to screw in a light bulb?
— Five. One to screw in the light bulb and four to share the experience.

How many Italians does it take to change a light bulb?
— Two. One to change it and one to sprinkle it with Parmesan.

How many psychologists does it take to change a light bulb?
— None. The bulb will change itself when it is ready.

How many psychologists does it take to change a light bulb?
— Just one, but the light bulb has to really WANT to change.

How many pessimists does it take to change a light bulb?
— None. Why bother? It's just going to burn out anyway.

25B Ha, ha, ha!

How to use a lift

Reading and listening

1 🔊 **The article is recorded.** (2 minutes 30 seconds)

2 🔊 **Students will need to hear this at least twice.**

Transcript 2 minutes 20 seconds
Presenter: Listen to two Americans in an elevator.

Ted: I just hate elevators. They bore me to my boots.

Bill:	*whistles*
Ted:	Ah!
Bill:	Yeah?
Ted:	Th…th…there must be some fun things you can do in an elevator, there must be! Must be.
Bill:	Yeah, OK, er . . . On a long ride . . .
Ted:	Right?
Bill:	Sway side to side while the elevator is moving.
Ted:	Oh, that's great! That's great!
Bill:	Yeah.
Ted:	Oh! How about…um…open your briefcase or bag, and while looking inside ask: 'Got enough air in there?' Haha! . . . oh, yeah.
Bill:	Hey, offer name tags to everyone getting on the elevator. Wear yours upside-down.
Ted:	How about if you just stood silent and motionless in the corner, facing the wall, without getting off, ever.
Bill:	Greet everyone getting on the elevator . . . with a warm handshake, then ask them to call you 'Admiral'.
Ted:	Very good, very good. You need a hat though. Oh, meow occasionally.
Bill:	Oh, that's good.
Ted:	Meow! Haha!
Bill:	Yeah, um…ask each passenger getting on if you can push the button for them.
Ted:	Oh, that's good. Haha. 'Can I push the button?'
Bill:	Oh yeah.
Ted:	Oh, say 'Ding!' on every floor.
Bill:	Lean against the button panel.
Ted:	Very nice, very nice . . . Ah . . . ah. Oh, how about if you…if you…if you went, 'I wonder what all these do?', then push all the red buttons.
Bill:	Yes.
Ted:	That's good.
Bill:	Make explosion noises when anyone presses a button . . .
Ted:	Oh, right. (*Explosion noise*)
Bill:	. . . including the red ones.
Ted:	Excellent!
Bill:	Um…take a chair into the elevator and sit on it . . . It's simple.
Ted:	Ohh.
Bill:	Say 'Have a good day' to everyone who gets off.
Ted:	Oh, that would be brilliant.
Bill:	Yeah.
Ted:	Oh, i…it's my floor.
Bill:	'Have a good day!'
Ted:	Stop that.
Bill:	Sorry.

3   **Expand the pairs into groups.**

Editing your work

1-2 👥 then 👥 + 👥

Suggested cuts

~~Here's a story which must be true because I read it in a newspaper. The report was about the Falkland Islands, which are a group of islands in the South Atlantic. According to the report, the pilots of the Royal Air Force who are stationed on the Falkland Islands are very bored with having nothing to do but fly from island to island.~~ These RAF pilots who are stationed on the Falkland Islands have invented a great game to make them feel less bored. ~~They have noticed that~~ The local penguins are fascinated by planes and always look up when one flies overhead. So the pilots look for a beach where there are lots of penguins standing together, and they fly along the beach from left to right ~~at the water's edge. They are delighted to see~~ Ten thousand penguins turning their heads in unison watching the planes go by. Then the pilots turn around and fly back from right to left and the penguins turn their heads in the opposite direction. The penguins behave like spectators at a slow-motion tennis match. Then ~~when the penguins on the beach have watched the planes fly in both directions,~~ the pilots fly out to sea ~~away from the penguins.~~ Then they fly back towards the beach, directly towards the penguins on the beach. As they fly over the beach, the penguins' heads go up, up, up – and ten thousand penguins fall over gently onto their backs. ~~The story must be true because I read it in a newspaper.~~

3 ✎ In the FCE exam compositions must be 120 to 180 words long. If they are longer, the examiners may stop reading after 180 words and miss your punch line.

Telling stories

1 👥 Oh no! Not more funny stories?
Yes, more penguins in **Activity 39** and a story about a dog in **Activity 7**.

2 👥 Students prepare their own stories . . .

3 👥 + 👥 . . . then join another pair to tell their stories.

That's all folks!

Hope you've had fun.

Teacher:	Max, describe a synonym.
Student:	A word you use when you can't spell the other word.

Teacher:	Can you spell 'caterpillar'?
Student:	How long do I have?
Teacher:	Why?
Student:	I want to wait until he changes into a butterfly. I can spell that.

21–25 Revision

Topic vocabulary

21 21 words from Unit 21

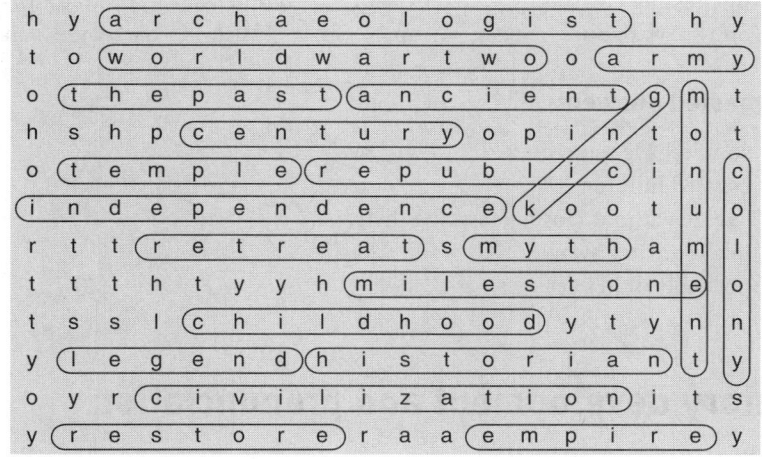

23 Words from Unit 23

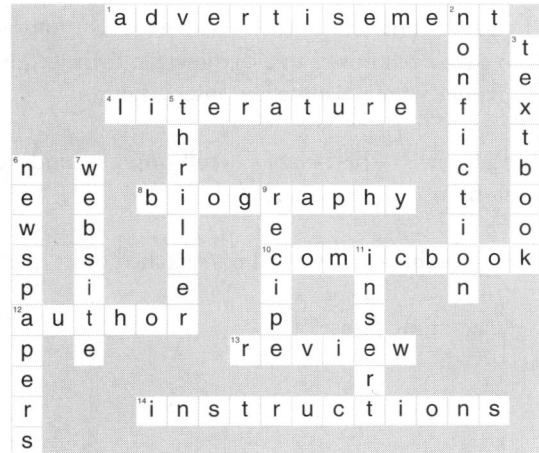

24 24 adjectives from Unit 24

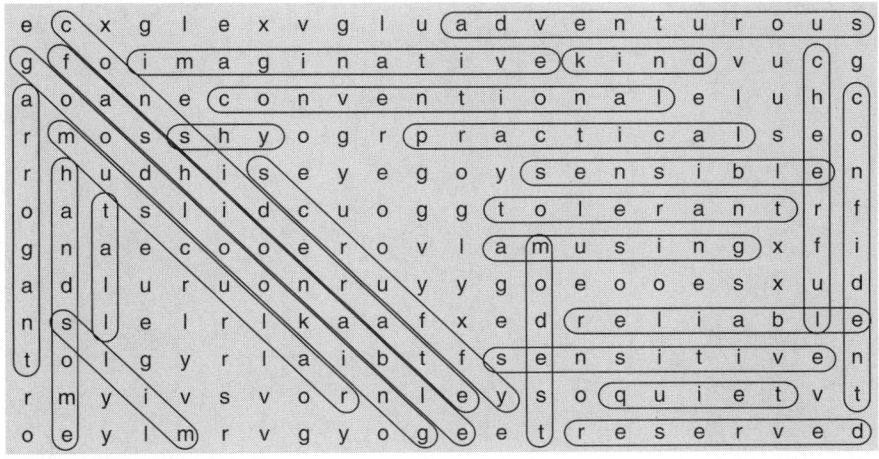

(actually there are 25 words here!)

Grammar review

A Suggested answers

21 might/must have   might/could/may have been   must/might have
22 At   on   from   in   after   in   to
23 by pressing   setting   to explain   to find out   by reading
24 off   away/out   back   up   for   back   back/by   in   out

B Suggested answers

21 should have remembered
22 blamed him for
23 sneeze without closing/shutting their
24 taken my bag away
25 probably didn't get

Vocabulary development and pronunciation

Suggested answers

21 sarcastically   angrily   nervously   kindly/apologetically

22 This week I read in the paper about two workers who were sent to prison for stealing their boss's car, a couple who gave a red flower to every guest at their wedding, and one article about the right way to reduce your waistline and lose weight.

23 absent-minded   brand-new   first-class   full stop   kind-hearted   left-handed police station   old-fashioned   reading list

24 went into   took off   sat back   turned on/switched on

25 Sit!   Next please!   at a time please!